**CCH BUSINESS OWNER'S TOOLKIT**™

# FIND & KEEP CUSTOMERS

## FOR YOUR SMALL BUSINESS

A *CCH Business Owner's Toolkit*™ Publication

Edited by Joanne Y. Cleaver

**CCH** INCORPORATED
Chicago

Cover designed by Tim Kaage, Laurel Graphx, Inc.

Books may be purchased at quantity discounts for educational, business or sales promotion use. For more information please contact:

Small Office Home Office Group
CCH INCORPORATED
2700 Lake Cook Road
Riverwoods, Illinois 60015

ISBN 0-8080-0354-2

Printed in the United States of America

# THE CCH BUSINESS OWNER'S TOOLKIT™ TEAM

**Joanne Y. Cleaver** has nearly 20 years of experience covering business, marketing and work-at-home issues as an author and freelance writer. In addition to being a weekly contributor to *Crain's Chicago Business*, she has penned numerous articles for *Home Office Computing*, *Small Office Computing*, *Working Woman* and *Marketing News*, as well as for various major metropolitan newspapers. Joanne is the author of the book, *Work from Home Options*, and holds journalism degrees from Northwestern University.

**Alice Magos** has over 35 years of experience running the operations of numerous small businesses. She is the author of the *CCH Business Owner's Toolkit*™ online advice column "Ask Alice." Alice is a popular instructor at small business seminars on accounting, financial planning and using the Internet; is an accountant and a Certified Financial Planner; and holds degrees from Washington University in St. Louis and Northwestern University.

**John L. Duoba** has 12 years of small business experience in book and magazine publishing, fulfilling various roles in editorial and production management. He has been involved in the publication of scores of titles, with multiple editions and issues raising the total well into the hundreds. John is a professional journalist and holds a degree from Northwestern University's Medill School of Journalism.

**Joel Handelsman** has 21 years of experience writing about business, tax and financial topics. He has experience with multiple new product and business ventures in the publishing industry, and has held a variety of management positions. Joel is an attorney and holds degrees from Northwestern University and DePaul University.

**Susan M. Jacksack** is frequently quoted as a small business expert in national publications including *The Wall Street Journal*, *The New York Times*, *Money* and *Worth*, and has made several guest appearances to discuss small business issues on CNBC. She has over 14 years of experience advising and writing for small business owners and consumers on tax, personal finance and other legal topics, and has conducted seminars for new and prospective entrepreneurs on tax issues, business planning and employment law. Susan is an attorney and a graduate of the University of Illinois, Urbana-Champaign.

**Martin Bush** has 15 years of experience providing legal, financial and tax advice to small and large businesses in various industries. He is a frequently quoted small business expert and has appeared on CNBC and National Public Radio. Martin is an attorney and a CPA, and holds degrees from Indiana University, DePaul University and Northwestern University.

We also would like to acknowledge the significant efforts Ron Hirasawa, who contributed greatly to this book.

In addition, we would like to thank Drew Snider for his contributions in the production of this book.

## PREFACE

So you have a concept for a new product or service. Your friends, neighbors and family members all tell you what a great idea it is and that you should start your own business. You decide to take the entrepreneurial plunge.

Or maybe you are already running your own business, and you want to increase sales or branch out into a new market, to boost the bottom line. You believe your plans for the future are a perfect fit for your current operation, and everybody urges you to seize the moment and quickly move forward.

Your supporters all say: Don't worry about how you are going to find customers that will be interested in buying it, how you are going to price it, or how you are going to get it into their hands. Instead, they insist: Focus on making the best product you can and, according to conventional wisdom, customers will buy and keep coming back.

This "Field of Dreams" approach runs a close second to the lack of a business plan as the reason most business ventures fail. An entrepreneur must have a marketing mindset before beginning to create that first product or to expand operations. Otherwise, it is almost a certainty that you will stand or sit by the door, phone, desk or computer waiting for customers who never show up.

Perhaps even more difficult than attracting customers is keeping them happy. We live in a highly competitive marketplace where consumers have hundreds and thousands of choices. Successful entrepreneurs nurture their relationships with their customers everyday, because they understand that the most effective way to get more business is from current customers.

*Find & Keep Customers for Your Small Business* guides small business owners through the entire marketing cycle of successfully creating and keeping new customers. It provides hundreds of practical tips, examples and ideas to help you understand your buyer's needs and wants; set prices to maximize revenue and profitability; choose distribution methods; and create attention-getting advertisements, promotions and packaging.

Why should you turn to us? **CCH INCORPORATED** is a leading provider of information and software to the business and professional community. More than four generations of business advisors have trusted our products, and now you can too.

A caution and an invitation — the discussions contained in this book are current as of the date of publication. But remember, things change. To keep abreast of the latest news affecting your business, visit *CCH*

*Business Owner's Toolkit*™ on the Internet (www.toolkit.cch.com) or on America Online (keyword: CCH).

While you're there, take a look at the other interactive information and tools we offer to assist you in running your business. You can also ask follow-up questions of our team of small business experts. We welcome and look forward to your questions and comments

**Martin Bush**

**Publisher, Small Office Home Office Group**

# Table of Contents

## Table of Contents

# Part I

# Developing a Marketing Mindset

This is the true tale of The Man Who Marketed Too Much. He had a good idea. Sick of the corporate rat race, he wanted to leverage his extensive hobby knowledge of video and multimedia equipment and production processes to launch a new company. He'd be his own boss, scripting, producing, editing and delivering videos and CDs for corporations. Besides, starting his own company would allow him to write off the tens of thousands of dollars he'd spent on cameras, microphones, sound mixers and editing equipment.

There was only one problem—clients. He didn't have any. Getting customers was something that the "other guys" had always done in his prior job as a corporate communications project manager. Then, there was always plenty to do—think up ways to showcase his employer's growing market presence, new products, awards. Someone else created the work by getting all those new customers. Not him.

So he had to figure out marketing and selling. He created a web site with lots of gee-whiz animation. He told people he had lots of video editing equipment. He called local companies asking if they had any video projects hanging around waiting to be made. He waited for the phone to ring.

Unfortunately, that was the sum total of the marketing efforts of this would-be entrepreneur. He never got any clients—and he never did figure out why.

Marketing is far more than simply running some ads and sponsoring the Boy Scouts' float at the Fourth of July parade. Successful marketers are constantly conversing with current and potential customers about how they're doing, what problems they're trying to solve, and what challenges they're setting for themselves. When you offer to customers products and services that meet or exceed their hopes, you've launched a successful marketing dialogue. The more of those dialogues you have, the more successful your company will be.

Part I lays the groundwork for developing a marketing mindset that will help you establish successful long-term relationships with customers.

*Chapter 1: The Marketing Challenge* paints the picture in broad strokes. You'll learn how to take your intriguing ideas and start to determine how they might be translated into saleable products or services.

*Chapter 2: Analyzing the Market Environment* outlines the key forces that you'll be contending with as you look for effective ways to bring your concept to market.

*Chapter 3: Finding Your Target Market* equips you to find the most effective and profitable section of the market where you can dig in and stake a claim.

*Chapter 4: Building a Plan To Reach Your Market* shows you how to analyze the information you've collected and to communicate with the buyers most likely to use your product or service.

# Chapter 1

# Overview: The Marketing Challenge

Chances are, you're already a whiz at marketing. If you've ever persuaded a spouse to rent the video *you* want to see, convinced a group of dubious volunteers that, yes, they can have fun painting fences outside the elementary school on a beautiful spring morning, or cajoled a group of skeptical employees to give your new time-management plan a shot, you've successfully applied marketing techniques.

Marketing isn't just a matter of telling someone that they should buy your product or service, and then bracing yourself for a crush of eager, cash-waving customers.

It *is* understanding what your potential customers and clients want to achieve by buying your product or service, and then structuring all elements of your operation—from developing products to setting the right price to creating a brand image to gracefully handling complaints—to meet or exceed those expectations.

That's a lot of balls to juggle, but if you didn't already have a sense of what your market wants and how you'll fill its needs, you wouldn't be launching or running a business. You can be your own best market researcher simply by constantly listening to your market and evaluating what you detect. Market research, pricing, packaging, distribution, advertising and promotion all fit into the picture, but a marketing plan is more than the sum of these parts. We'll dig into the specifics of each of these projects in the rest of this book. This chapter's devoted to the big picture.

Most people instinctively employ classic marketing techniques every day. They're constantly surveying their work, neighborhood, home and social environments for signs of change, and then immediately speculating about how that change might affect them. Is that unfamiliar woman you just greeted in the elevator the new corporate controller? She seemed nice—maybe you can get to know her over coffee and donuts, and see if she's open to buying those ergonomic chairs that your department has been campaigning for. When thoughts like these run through your mind, you've sized up the market climate for your request and quickly framed an approach that might gain attention and credibility for your proposal. That's marketing.

The process is similar, but the stakes are considerably higher, when you're shaping your company's marketing strategy. Assuming that you're in business for the long haul, you'll want to look at immediate and emerging market conditions for the products or services you want to sell. That involves figuring out who your competitors are (and will be) and developing a sixth sense for how economic trends are likely to affect your customers.

You'll use all this great information to develop products or services that the meet specific needs of your customers, and to communicate how your products or services are unique from your competitors'— and thus worthy of your customers' money, effort and loyalty.

There are five questions that every business needs to ask itself as it defines its market and its place in it:

- **What's unique** about your business idea? The fact that you are the one who thought it up isn't enough, unless your Mom comprises your entire market. What specific attributes— price, timeliness, quality, style, rarity—does your product have that others don't?

- **Who is your target buyer?** Who buys your product or service (or similar ones) now? Are you making enough of a profit selling to your current customers? Do you want to attract a different type of client? Why?

- **Who are your competitors?** Can you effectively compete in your chosen market with the resources you have on hand now and are reasonably likely to acquire?

- **What positioning message** do you want to communicate to your target buyers? How can you position your business or product to let people know you are special, in ways that are important to these buyers?

- **What's your distribution strategy?** How will you get your product or service in the hands of your customers? Often your distribution method will provide an additional marketing channel, especially if the timeliness or distinction of your delivery channel separates you from your competitors.

# WHAT'S YOUR UNIQUE BUSINESS IDEA?

Intuitively, or based on sound research, you believe your business will succeed because you are doing something different from some or all of your competitors.

An **inherent difference** is one that you can demonstrate or prove to customers.

Some inherent differences are quantitative, or easily measured. It's easy for customers to quantify your claim that you sell the cheapest canned food in town. All they have to do to is read your competitors' ads to see if you're meeting or beating the price on a six-ounce can of soup that week.

Inherent differences can also be qualitative, or linked to the quality of your product, service or knowledge.

For instance, your distinguishing characteristic might be the unique expertise you've gained at a corporate job—expertise you want to use as a launching pad for a consulting practice. Let's say that you're the most organized records warehouse supervisor that the company has ever had (at least, according to your current boss). Not only do you make sure employees get the old files that they request quickly, and make sure that those files are promptly returned to their proper slots, but you've also been assertively learning about e-mail, as well as new ways to store and retrieve files and data through computers, laser discs and scanners.

You might leverage your experience to position yourself as an independent consultant who helps companies figure out mailroom bottlenecks and choose new technologies to solve them. It's the quality of the "been-there, done-that" advice you give your new clients that distinguishes you from data retrieval specialists who've never actually managed a records warehouse.

It's more difficult to prove the value of a **perceived difference** to potential customers. A perceived difference is one that may be linked to inherent differences, but is largely created through marketing efforts. We'll talk more in Chapter 5 about creating a brand; suffice it to say here that all the assumptions and associations that people make about a brand are created by the differences that its marketers try to create around it, often separate from actual product attributes and results. Are name-brand canned peach slices actually better tasting, more nutritious and prettier than store-brand peaches? No....but the lush, flavorful image of the name-brand peaches is cultivated by artful ads while the store-brand peaches must sit on the shelf in lonely contrast, attractive only for their price.

## Case Study — Armitage Hardware (part 1)

 *For decades, Armitage Hardware, a member of the ACE hardware cooperative, occupied a cozy spot niche in its Chicago neighborhood. It carried a huge selection of the usual hardware store stuff, from nails to dishpans to gizmos guaranteed to keep squirrels off your birdfeeders.*

*What distinguished Armitage from nearby hardware stores was the owners' uncanny ability to detect and create custom solutions for offbeat niches. Not only did the store provide a glazier service to fix broken windows, but customers could also order heavy, finished-to-order plate-glass tops for coffee tables.*

*President (and son of the store's founder) Brian O'Donnell listened when a retail customer complained about the hassles he was having managing all the household details for a clutch of housing units owned by local company. Visiting executives were supposed to be able to step right into a fully equipped household, but nagging annoyances like replacing mildewed shower curtains were driving the retail customer to distraction. O'Donnell worked up a proposal for an Armitage manager to coordinate acquisition, installation, maintenance and replacement of all the soft goods, from linens to mixing bowls, for the housing units. The customer loved the idea and Armitage made a tidy sum on the project—which also led to a lucrative branch business selling industrial supplies to customers like local plumbers.*

*Armitage's market positioning statement could have been "The Can-Do Store."*

*It wasn't just what it did, but how it did it, that endeared Armitage to its neighborhood retail customers. O'Donnell and his managers often set up grills on the sidewalk outside their store and cooked nonstop on spring weekends to demonstrate the features of the latest line of Weber Grills. They'd treat any passerby to a hamburger or a plate of ribs, hot off the grill. Weekend warriors could attend classes on everything from installing locks to repairing sink traps. The store was a mecca for the ambitious rehabbers who populate its yuppified neighborhood.*

*O'Donnell says that his philosophy of researching customers' needs has always been to pay close attention to customer comments. He had plenty of chances to do that as he worked with them side-by-side on neighborhood projects. He also knew that his target customers wanted to know all their options before they settled on one, so he always carried as many SKU's (stock keeping units) as possible. "Every time my family goes on vacation, I go into hardware stores just to see what they have," he says. "I never find one that has a complete selection (of any manufacturer's line). I always thought that if we offered that, people would come to us."*

*Things were going along swimmingly for Armitage until the fall of 1995. That's when Ace executives told O'Donnell that he'd better brace himself: a Home Depot hardware superstore was set to open just a few blocks away, in just a few months. It was tempting, but naïve, to hope that savvy Armitage customers would reject the super-low prices and vast selection offered up by Home Depot. Ace told O'Donnell to batten down the hatches for a sales dip of at least 5 percent. Customers would probably flirt with the new store for upwards of 18 months before returning to the place where they could get a fair price and lots of hand-holding and product recommendations.* (continued on page 12)

How different is different enough? It's not realistic to think that you'll be the only player in your market category—unless it's so tiny that it can only support one company. Once word gets out that you've cultivated a profitable product or service, others will horn in. Or you may be entering an already-crowded market and seeking to differentiate yourself not because you're offering something completely unique, but because you have an attractive price, quality, breadth of service or product line, or some other characteristic. Just as your competitors will borrow some of your successful techniques, you'll no doubt borrow some of theirs.

Of course, if your market is limited geographically, you can adopt ideas that have worked successfully for similar businesses in other geographic areas. Franchisees within the same system do this all the time, and often relay news of their successful marketing brainstorms to other franchisees through company newsletters and online bulletin boards. (In fact, Ronald McDonald was created by a single McDonald's Corporation store owner, and look how far he got.)

Meanwhile, you'll need to constantly keep one eye focused on your marketing objectives: When all is said and done, how do you want people to think of your company? As the biggest, the best, the one with the most style, the friendliest, or some combination of attributes? All other marketing decisions must support your objectives.

If you start to veer off in another direction, or simply experiment with a series of unrelated campaigns and promotions, most potential customers will be confused. Advertising speedy delivery one month, then stressing a super repair service the next month, could confuse potential customers of an office equipment leasing company. Should a customer choose the company because it will deliver a new copier 24 hours after the lease is signed, or because it guarantees that stalled copiers will be fixed the same day that you place the service call? Unless you build a clear, compelling image, people won't know what to expect from your company. And if they don't know what to expect, they're unlikely to spend their money to find out.

## Work Smart

Marketing **objectives** crystallize the results that you want to ultimately reap from your cumulative marketing efforts: "To be the dominant supplier of packaging to cosmetics manufacturers east of the Mississippi, while maintaining a 15 percent gross margin."

A marketing **strategy** is the bird's-eye-view roadmap of how you'll achieve that objective: "To become a supplier to the top five cosmetics manufacturers within the next five years while building a reputation for quality within our segment of the packaging industry."

*A marketing* **plan** *outlines specific steps that you'll take, often within a specified schedule, to achieve various points in the strategy: "This year, we will identify three dominant and three fast-growing cosmetics manufacturers and gain contracts from them."*

*Marketing* **goals** *break down the plan into short-term projects: "Within the next three months, we will conduct research to identify the three dominant cosmetics manufacturers, find out how satisfied they are with their current packaging suppliers, learn what expansion or product line-revision plans they have and when they might entertain serious proposals from new suppliers; and determine who makes the decision to try out a new packaging contractor."*

## Creating a Unique Positioning Statement

To weave together the unique market elements that your company offers, you'll need to carefully shape a **market positioning statement**. All marketing decisions should be measured against the positioning statement: How does this effort support it? Does this effort contradict it? The smaller your marketing budget, the more important it is to have a laser-like positioning statement. By sticking to it, you're much less likely to waste money on fuzzy-headed projects that sap money and energy, but do nothing to bring business in the door.

Here are some steps to help you crystallize the unique benefits your company will offer customers. In twenty-five or fewer words, how is your business different? Express it in terms that will serve as the underlying message of all your advertising, promotions, sales communications and other marketing activities. This isn't an advertising slogan that's used on everything from T-shirts to giveaway mugs. Rather, the positioning statement is a tool to help you focus on what your business is all about.

What is unique about your business or brand compared to direct competitors? Here are some questions to consider:

1. Which of these factors are most important to the buyers and end users of your business or brand?

2. Which of these factors are not easily imitated by competitors?

3. Which of these factors can be easily communicated and understood by buyers or end users?

4. Can you construct a memorable message of these unique, meaningful qualities about your business or brand?

5. Finally, how will you communicate this message to buyers and end users? Marketing tools include media advertising, promotion programs (e.g., direct mail), packaging and sales personnel.

*Stuck? It can be hard to articulate a gut feeling. Try discussing your business concept with partners, marketing-savvy friends and your spouse.*

*If after reflection and brainstorming, you still haven't put your finger on your market positioning statement, try identifying the positioning statement of your most direct competitors.*

*If you still can't pinpoint yours, you may want to reconsider your business concept. Is it really as distinctive as you thought?*

If you've been in business for a while, you may have intuitively constructed a positioning statement. For example, if you decided to provide free delivery service to your customers because *no one else* in town is doing it, you've constructed a statement based on service that you are communicating to the intended target buyer. If, however, you offer free delivery service because *everyone else* in town does so and you need to provide it simply to keep up with the competition, it's not something that sets you apart and should not be the focus of your statement.

## What's It Worth to Your Customers?

Even if you have the snappiest marketing positioning statement ever conceived, you'll be in and out of business in a flash if you're marketing a product or service that hardly anyone wants, needs or understands. Your positioning statement may be unique, but you also need to promote a difference that will motivate potential customers to prefer your offerings rather than your competitors'. Will enough people want that unique difference that they'll pay? How much will they pay? Even if you're a veteran in your industry, you'll benefit from an arm's-length look at the market environment and how your business concept fits in to that market. Specifically, you're looking for a unique need that's not currently being filled…that you can profitably fill.

In order to be able to accurately determine whether your business idea has enough appeal to a sufficient number of customers, you'll have to get in touch with your target buyers.

## DEFINE YOUR TARGET BUYER

Do you know precisely who your customers are? You may know many of them by name, but do you really know what type of people or businesses they are?

If you sell to consumers, do you have **demographic information** (e.g., their average income ranges, education, typical occupations, geographic location, family makeup, etc.) that identifies your target buyer? What about **lifestyle information** (e.g., hobbies, interests, recreational/entertainment activities, political beliefs, cultural practices, etc.) on your target buyer?

If your products or services are geared to other businesses, are you up to speed on economic, technological, operational and other trends affecting their market milieu?

This type of information can help you both adapt your products and services to match the actual needs of your customers, and also point the way to the appropriate advertising, promotional and media channels that will reach them most effectively.

## Potential Pitfall

*Make sure you're figuring out the needs of the people who will be spending their own money on the product. You might end up advertising to the ultimate user of the product as well, but don't confuse the two. Chocolate cookie breakfast cereal is marketed directly to children, the ultimate users (we hope), but the actual target buyers are the children's parents.*

*While ads may generate an excitement in the children for the cereal, it's a rare parent who won't at least take a cursory glance at the box to check that there's a shred of nutritional value in the stuff. And, if it's too expensive, parents won't buy it no matter how much Junior whines. Successful cereal marketers address parents' concerns as well as the kids' cravings.*

Here are two helpful ways to analyze your market to better understand what motivates your customers to seek out and buy services and products like yours—identifying a niche market and segmenting your market.

# Niche Marketing

Most businesses find that as much as 80 percent of their sales comes from a very dedicated base of repeat customers. When you find out what particularly attracts these customers to your company's products or services, you're well on your way to defining your niche market. Then you can pour additional marketing and product development resources into cultivating additional sales from your repeat buyers, identifying additional buyers with the same need profile, and learning from these customers what additional products and sales you can develop for them.

This loyal base will provide the steady sales, cash flow, and ultimately, the profits that enable you to grow your company. Before you simply label any big subgroup of customers as your core market, first consider:

- Can you measure the size, profitability and annual growth rate of this industry through industry and governmental reports and other sources?

- Is this subgroup substantial enough to generate planned sales volume?

- Can you reach these customers efficiently through your company's distribution methods?

- Are they likely to be persuaded through the types of advertising and promotional efforts that you believe you can afford?

Pair this information with key factors that you face in winning loyal customers in this subgroup:

- How strong are direct competitors?

- What indirect competitors might nibble away at the size of the market?

- How similar are yours' and your competitors' products in the buyers' minds? Do they detect an inherent difference? Would they be persuaded by one?

- What new products may competitors soon introduce?

- How easy is it for new competitors to enter the market? Can you protect your products or services via copyright, patent or other legal means to slow the emergence of new competitors?

Take your core market for granted at your own peril. Consumers and businesses are constantly bombarded with new products, new services and new ways of solving perennial problems. Once you've won those customers' loyalty, you'll have to continue to earn it.

It is also important to be able to identify and estimate the size of your target market, particularly if you're thinking about a new venture, so that you can tell if the customer base is large enough to support your business or new product idea. Remember that it's not enough that people like your business concept. There must be enough target buyers on a frequent-enough basis to sustain your company sales, spending and profits from year to year. For instance, selling a product or service that people may need only once in a lifetime (e.g., an indestructible toothbrush) may not be a sustainable business, unless a large number of people need it at any given time, or everyone needs it eventually (e.g., funeral services).

## Case Study — Armitage Hardware (part II)

*In characteristic style, O'Donnell refused to be spooked by the imminent invasion of Home Depot on his turf. This could be a golden opportunity to distinguish Armitage not only from other mom-and-pop hardware stores, but from the giant everything-to-everybody stores as well. What product or service could he introduce that would belong uniquely to Armitage and separate it from the crush of other retailers that carried many of the same goods (from mass discounters to upscale mail-order catalogs)?*

*O'Donnell's learned skill of listening carefully to customer comments and coming up with imaginative solutions to their problems paid off, big-time. Noodling on the idea that consumers would be attracted to the complete selection offered by any one line of products or goods, he hit gold: Why not push the store's relationship with some key suppliers up several notches?*

*As an experiment in the fall of 1995, O'Donnell hired an Internet web site designer to create a web site that would showcase every single item produced by the Weber-Stephens Co., makers of that suburban backyard classic, the Weber Grill. He would have in stock, all the time, every color, size and variation of the Weber grill. He reserved the web address (URL) www.webergrills.com, and hired and trained three new employees to answer questions about the grills, to explain how Armitage would provide replacement parts and service of every kind to current grill owners, and to take orders for the grills and accessories showcased on the site.*

*Only after all that was done did O'Donnell call the Weber-Stephens executives to let them know what he'd done. He admits he went out on a limb by pouring resources into the site without getting their permission—not to mention the audacity of grabbing their logical web address for Armitage. But his bravado served to get the immediate and intense attention of Weber-Stephens executives. They wanted to know what he was up to.*

*O'Donnell explained his proposition—as the Internet grew, Weber-Stephens would inevitably be inundated with questions from consumers and inquiries about buying Weber-Stephens products. Did the company really want to field all those e-mails on its own, and set up an e-commerce site that would directly compete with its carefully nurtured network of retailers? No, it did not. So, why not let Armitage serve as the de facto "official" sales site? Armitage committed to carrying every single item that Weber made and also agreed to handle customers and promotions in a way that was consistent with Weber's corporate image, and the Weber-Stephens executives agreed to let the web experiment play out. (continued on page 16)*

# Segmenting Your Market

As your company grows, several distinct core markets may emerge. You'll want to evaluate the profitability of each before staking significant resources on those segments. Some segments may develop into parallel core markets, or you may decide from the outset to formulate different marketing strategies for distinctly different market segments. This works if they complement themselves somehow, even if that fit is only one that makes sense within the context of your company. Halloween pumpkins, Christmas trees and flats of flowering plants only have in common that they're all perishable goods with strong seasonal appeal. Many retail stores, nurseries and farm stands successfully segue from one seasonal specialty to the next, year-round, with the same homeowners returning to them for pumpkins, Christmas trees and flowers to plant in their spring beds.

You may find that you have a particular flair for serving a segment of a very large market—say, manufacturing short runs of replacement parts for outdated but still functioning electronic equipment instead of mass producing components for currently popular electronics. Or you might corral one segment of a large market based on demographics, lifestyle or buying preferences, or another shared characteristic.

For example, you might divide up your customers by age group and find that you sell most of your products to people aged 18 to 34. You might divide them up by family size and find that you sell most of your products to married couples with young children. You might divide them up by economic status and find that you sell most products to people with an annual income of about $50,000 to $100,000. You might divide them up by geographic location and find that you sell most of your products to people living within two specific zip codes.

Many small businesses stop there, thinking they have enough information to be able to identify and communicate with their most likely customers. However, savvy companies push on and find out even more information about their customers' lifestyles, values, life stage and buying preferences.

## Work Smart

*Let's define some terms:*

**Demographics** *refer to age, sex, income, education, race, martial status, size of household, geographic location, size of city and profession.*

**Psychographics** *refer to personality and emotionally based behavior linked to purchase choices; for example, whether customers are risk-takers or risk-avoiders, impulsive buyers, etc.*

**Lifestyle** *refers to the collective choice of hobbies, recreational pursuits, entertainment, vacations, and other non-work time pursuits*

**Belief and value systems** *include religious, political, nationalistic, and cultural beliefs and values.*

**Life stage** *refers to chronological benchmarking of people's lives at different ages (e.g., pre-teens, teenagers, empty-nesters, etc.).*

How can you find out more about your customers? Through market research, that's how. Big companies segment their markets by conducting extensive market research projects, consisting of several rounds of exploratory research:

1.  **Customer and product data collection** — Researchers gather data from users of similar products on:

    — number and timing of brand purchases

    — reasons for purchases

    — consumers' attitudes about various product attributes

    — importance of the product to the lifestyle of consumer

    — category user information (demographics, psychographics, media habits, etc.)

2.  **Factor and cluster analysis** — Researchers analyze the data collected on customers and products to find correlations between product purchases and other factors, as a basis for identifying actionable consumer target clusters. Clusters are defined as niche markets, where there are identifiable numbers of buyers or users who share the same characteristics and who thus can be reached by adept advertising and promotion. Senior citizens in Minneapolis may have a particular fondness for cruising the Caribbean in February.

3.  **Cluster identification and importance ranking** — Researchers then determine:

    — whether clusters are large and viable enough to spend marketing funds on them

    — whether potential marketing niche clusters fit strategic company objectives; i.e., does marketing to this group fit your market positioning statement and marketing objectives?

**How do you segment your market into bite-sized pieces?** You can keep up with trade journals, research general business trends through publication such as *The Wall Street Journal* and *Business Week*, subscribe to customized online news services, and trawl trade shows to keep up with the market segments you've identified. It may be worth your while to individually question key trade buyers or pay the $6,000 or so it costs to assemble a consumer focus group to hear your customers' perceptions of your niche.

Don't forget to track your competitors' moves—big companies often announce what they're going to do or new products they're going to introduce, then roll them out gradually. That gives smaller competitors plenty of advance warning to create and present even more attractive products and services to the same market segment.

Online databases provided by trade groups, trade magazines, various federal government agencies, and advocacy groups can also be mined for valuable clues about market segments. You can also buy, for prices ranging from $25 to $1,000+, research reports on current trends in your target segments from research giants such as A.C. Nielsen, Burke, Information Resources Inc., and Forrester Research.

# WHO ARE YOUR COMPETITORS?

Once you've identified what's unique about your business and who your target buyers are, you need to take a good, long look at your competition.

Identifying your **direct competitors** is important before you dive in headfirst to your new market segment. The more you know, the less risk, time and resources you'll waste on segments that aren't a good fit.

For example, a new salty snack chip product may have a unique taste, texture, appearance and health benefits. But effectively competing with every salty snack (both direct competitors like salty chips and indirect competitors like popcorn, salty nuts—not to mention non-salty snack foods like cookies and candy) is difficult, even for a large, successful snack food company like Frito-Lay. If the competition is entrenched—and if it has pretty good products or services—you'll have a hard time breaking in.

With all these factors to consider, you may be tempted to just cut your prices and live with a lower profit margin. That might work, but be sure you've weighed the consequences before you sell yourself cheap.

## Competing Just on Price

Businesses based on the idea of providing less expensive products and services to customers often find themselves in cutthroat price wars. Customers attracted by price are also repelled by it. You can lose a customer over a 10-cent difference on a package of toilet paper or a $30 difference in the price of a coach airplane ticket.

You may find yourself wooing the same customers over and over again. After awhile, it may not be worth it. If you "lose money on every sale but make it up in volume," you're still losing money at the end of the year. Your operation may not have sufficient economies of scale to be able to sustain a permanent "always the lowest price" market position. And when customers are accustomed to extracting rock-bottom prices from you, it's awfully hard to persuade them that other product or service attributes are worth any extra money at all. As hard as you try to persuade them to trade up, your customers may just expect you to throw in upgrades and improvements for free.

The best protection for long-term success, where low price is a cornerstone of your product differentiation, is to:

- Be the first company to corner this low-price niche.

- Have an additional unique idea as the basis for your product or service.

- Surround low price with as many secondary sources of product and service differentiation with your competitors as possible. A dry cleaner may charge the lowest price for miles around for washing and pressing men's dress shirts, but make it up in charging market rates for dry cleaning, plus offer while-you-wait hem and sleeve alterations, for a premium price.

## Case Study — Armitage Hardware (part III)

*As O'Donnell continued to tweak www.webergrills.com, he became acutely aware of the trust that the Weber-Stephens executives were placing in him. Sure, they'd had a good supplier-retailer relationship before, but now, their entire brand reputation and how it was presented in the vast new world of Internet shopping were placed in his hands. He was not only marketing grills to customers, but had positioned himself as a champion and protector of the Weber brand as well.*

*"We have always treated our supplier relationship almost as a family-type relationship. We wouldn't exploit it. We could have put links to 'Beer across America,' to 'Cigars across America,' and they would have paid us for sales that came from our site. But we didn't want to associate alcohol and tobacco with Weber," he says. "I always put myself in their position. If there's anything on the site, like smokey chips or grill tools, besides Weber, it had to be top quality, and never competitive with Weber products. When we represent ourselves, we're representing them."*

*The Weber site launched in April, 1996, just as Home Depot opened. Armitage's retail customers were lured over to the big store—who wouldn't be? But while they explored the wide open aisles of Home Depot, O'Donnell was reveling in the immediate success of www.webergrills.com. The site immediately replaced revenue lost to customers who'd meandered over to Home Depot. And, curiously enough, O'Donnell found that the web site drew in hundreds of new neighborhood customers. They couldn't believe that they'd found just what they wanted at the site, and it was in stock down the block. Of course, while they were in the store, they'd usually pick up some grass seed, grab a hammer and get some paint mixed, too.*

*O'Donnell's strategy of partnering with a manufacturer with a strong brand following, and serving as that manufacturer's de facto retail web site, was easily transferred to other product categories. Before long, he had locked up sites for the pricey status-symbol Combi Italian baby strollers (www.combistrollers.com) and was shipping strollers all over the world. Next came all things Coleman, at www.colemanoutdoor.com, and every item made by multipurpose tool manufacturer Leatherman, at www.leathermangear.com. O'Donnell has made such a name for himself that he has started consulting to other small retailers to show them how they can duplicate the everything-in-a-narrow-niche strategy—a lucrative niche in itself.*

*Meanwhile, O'Donnell's enthusiasm for keeping up with the corporate property soft goods management project was fading. He coveted the store space devoted to glass finishing for more displays of what Armitage offered over the web. So he shut down the soft goods service and outsourced the glass finishing to a nearby glass specialty shop. Meanwhile, his brother, Kevin, decided to become the store's e-commerce maven and completely revamped the web site so that customers could complete their entire transactions online. Some still prefer to talk to a customer sales rep, and they can, through the store's toll-free phone number. But the efficiencies gained by automating the site freed up three employees to spend more time on the retail selling floor.*

*That floor's considerably larger. Having rearranged the space, O'Donnell has set up a 1,500 square foot "Internet Store" showcase to further underscore the store's unique offerings to its walk-in customers. Currently, online sales account for 9 percent of Armitage's annual revenue. "Our goal is to be the dominant retailer in the fields we choose—the biggest and best Leatherman, Coleman, Combi and Weber dealers in the country," says O'Donnell.*

# WHAT'S YOUR POSITIONING MESSAGE?

You know you're special. Your potential customers won't know until you tell them. And they won't care unless they can see how your special angle directly makes their lives easier. No matter how unusual your product idea, how mind-bending your service, how fair your price, you're just a person with some ideas until you net a paying customer.

Inherent differences are relatively easy to explain. Once you've told customers about the **features** of your products, explain the **benefits** to them of buying the product or using your service—exactly how that service or product will relieve an operational headache, fulfill a yearning, or in some other fashion fill a need that that customer has.

With your market positioning statement firmly in mind, you can slice out specific benefits that will distinguish your products and services in the market. **Differentiation** is the collection of differences in features and benefits versus competitive products. The key is to determine how important these collective differences are to buyers and then to communicate them to potential buyers.

Once you've pinpointed that meaningful difference, you can

consistently communicate it to your market through an entire arsenal of marketing tools, from distribution to packaging. All these elements need to coordinate in style, tone and message, to convey a consistent image of the meaningful difference that will motivate your target to actually buy. That image will also shape your target market's impression of your company.

## How To Strengthen Product Positioning

Even as your marketing efforts are taking off, listen carefully to current customers so that you can adapt your approach to meet their needs better and create additional products for them. When you unearth a product or service benefit that you weren't aware of, see how you can emphasize it in future advertising and promotional efforts. Include loyal customers in testing new products and services, and adjust your design, packaging, distribution and promotion accordingly.

### Potential Pitfall

Be careful not to **overposition**, or make promises about features and benefits that the product or business does not always deliver. Overpositioning can also mean making promises about product features and benefits that are not apparent to users/buyers. Don't promise to complete photo processing in an hour if all your machines, working at peak capacity, can only accommodate a few orders in 60 minutes.

Conversely, avoid **underpositioning**, or failing to describe all the features and benefits that the product or business delivers or has, or failing to describe distinctive product features and benefits that are apparent to users or buyers. You may not think that the "Grandma's Brag Book" photo albums you stock are much to write home about, but if your photo finishing shop is located near a retirement community, your most loyal customers may be smitten with the brag books. In that case, of course, you'll order brag books in all colors and start hosting "how to personalize your brag book" craft classes at the local senior citizens' center, right?

## WHAT'S YOUR DISTRIBUTION STRATEGY?

Part of the challenge of marketing is figuring out which distribution method to use. As soon as you decide which business or product category to compete in, distribution decisions must be made based upon what your competition is doing, what modes are readily available and affordable, and what technological trends may soon affect distribution in your industry.

Service businesses may or may not be subject to the same physical distribution limitations as product-based businesses. For example, financial planning services may be offered from printed material; be sold at retail; be sold by consultants face-to-face; or be delivered electronically by computer, by phone or by correspondence—a multitude of different distribution systems.

Distribution decisions have significant implications for:

- product margins and profits

- marketing budgets

- final retail pricing

- sales management practices

Distribution channels can include one or more of these options:

- **Retail** — stores selling to final consumer buyers (one store, or a chain of stores)

- **Wholesale** — an intermediary distribution channel that usually sells to retail stores

- **Direct mail** — generally, catalog merchants that sell directly to consumer buyers at retail prices plus shipping (e.g., Land's End, L.L. Bean) via mail

- **Telemarketing** — merchants selling directly to consumer buyers at retail via phones

- **Electronic commerce** — merchants selling directly to consumer buyers at retail prices, or business-to-business products and services sold over the Internet or proprietary online services such as America Online and CompuServe

- **Sales force** — salaried employees of a company, or independent commissioned representatives who usually sell products for more than one company

As your business grows, you'll become adept at picking up information from all the feedback channels available to you—core customers, new market segments, employees, your sales force, even chat rooms and listservs on the Internet. Integrating that information into your marketing strategy will become second nature. With a bit of planned luck, you'll soon be able to analyze the most conclusive measure of marketing success: the growth of your sales, profits and share of your target market.

# Chapter 2

# Analyzing the Market Environment

In order to sell your products or services, you've got to know your target market, inside and out. That's just as important for established, growing businesses as it is for startups. The last thing you want to do is pour money, time and effort into a venture that doesn't meet a market need or will be immediately crushed by powerful competitors.

Ultimately, your idea must fulfill a need for your buyers and must do so in a way that's somehow superior to the competition. If you want to be sure that your idea will do these two crucial things, you need to know as much as you can about the following:

- your competitors

- your target buyers

- the marketing environment

- market growth and trends

## YOUR COMPETITORS

New products and services are being introduced into the market more quickly than ever before, thanks to the heartbeat speed of electronic communications, ever-more-powerful and ever-cheaper computers, and brand-new ways of doing business, such as electronic commerce. Whatever room for error there used to be continues to shrink. Feared competitors may abruptly shift their strategies and exit your market, or they may develop a fresh approach and introduce services and products that you'd never thought of.

*Market research is an ongoing process, not a one-time project.* Fortunately, the

---

upside of the speed of modern communications means that you can dig out trends, market projections and information on your competitors much more easily and cheaply than ever before. (And they can do the same!)

In order to compete effectively, you need to know:

- Who are your competitors?

- What are your competitors' strengths and weaknesses?

- What are your competitors planning to do next?

- How do your competitors spend their marketing budgets?

# Who Are Your Competitors?

Your competitors are not always who you think they are. A careful analysis of your competition should include all available options for the buyers' spending dollar. And some of these options may not be direct competitors, but they are nonetheless siphoning off potential business from your company.

---

## Work Smart

*For example, if you are a manufacturer of popcorn products, your direct competitors are probably other brands of popcorn in the market. But what about tortilla chips, peanuts, snack mixes or potato chips? And what about rice cakes, candy bars, cake/pie items, rolled candy, gum or ice cream?*

*The target consumer may be choosing from an entire universe of junk food options when considering a snack—or the hungry consumer might figure that 4 p.m. is too close to dinner for a filling snack and simply opt for a can of cola.*

---

As you define your competition, you're also defining your own unique positioning statement. Your products or services might be more convenient, cheaper, of higher quality, more stylish, more readily available, or any combination of these and other selling points. You'll need to know how you stack up against the competition, point by unique selling point.

## Competitor Levels

It's helpful to break down your competitors by levels, ranging from your most direct competitors to those who are more remote.

- Most immediately obvious are your **direct competitors**— companies that offer products or services that reasonable buyers might think are just about the same as yours, and that are sold in your immediate market area. A garden center competes directly with other garden and home centers that carry a similar array of plants and gardening supplies and accessories, within a 10-mile radius.

- **Indirect competitors** aren't immediately obvious, but are serious competition nonetheless. They offer similar products and services in a slightly different product category—one that's relatively easily substituted for your category—or through a distribution channel different from yours but still convenient for your target buyers. Our garden center also competes with mail-order nurseries, from which you can shop from the comfort of your armchair, and landscape contractors that not only help you choose your plants, but put them in the ground, too. By tracking the moves of your indirect competitors, you may get early insight into important market trends that will soon directly impact your own category.

- **Tertiary competitors** are also going after the buyer, but offer a totally different option for that same dollar. Some gardeners in our center's market may have such a tough row to hoe that they all decide to pave over their plots; in that case, cement contractors become rather ominous competitors. Or, perhaps a contingent of hobby gardeners suddenly defects to birdwatching and diverts money previously spent on flower seed to birdseed.

The key thing to remember is that your target buyer has lots of options. Smart buyers explore as many as they feasibly can. That's why it's so important to shape your products or services right from the beginning to be distinctly different from your direct competitors.

### Case Study — Julie Longo & Associates, Inc.

*For more than 14 years, Julie Longo thrived on the fast pace and technological challenges she solved as a producer of technical and engineering videos for a huge aerospace manufacturer. By videotaping the process of making sections of large aircraft, the manufacturer created an archive of precisely how things were constructed.*

*Months before she decided to establish her own technical video production company, Longo started sizing up the market. While she'd been mainly focused on videos that would be used by other professionals in the business, she also knew that many companies were interested in producing videos of projects as public relations materials; for instance, a construction company might want to produce a children's educational video about building bridges. And, well-scripted videos can serve as powerful marketing tools at trade shows, as they can demonstrate a process that's impossible to re-create in a trade show booth.*

*Such videos aren't cheap, though: A bare-bones project runs $5,000, while a full-fledged half-hour documentary-type show can cost over $50,000. For most projects, there's only one chance to get each shot just right. And if the angle isn't right, or the most important procedures ignored, the client will look foolish instead of sophisticated.*

*Longo knew that marketing her new business, Julie Longo & Associates, Inc., would involve much more than standing in front of a camera reciting her resume. She subscribed to the most helpful of the video production journals that she'd had at her corporate job. And knowing that many defense contractors were branching out into other markets, she figured that she'd be able to gain jobs on a variety of topics from those same companies as they diversified.*

*New Jersey-based Longo hasn't got many direct competitors, but felt she needed to persuade cost-conscious companies to consider videos instead of assuming that they couldn't afford one, or that it would be too much hassle. She had to pinpoint her unique selling proposition and then figure out the best audience to receive that proposition. "Most technical companies are used to putting out high-end brochures and reports, but I've seen too many corporations hire video producers who consider style over content, and they don't get really into the details that the viewers want to know about and that the engineers want to communicate," she says.*

*Longo decided to concentrate on cultivating her personal credibility among a small, tight-knit universe—not of video producers, but of engineers and technical project managers. After all, they were the ones that would have budgetary authority to approve such a big-ticket project. She joined several local engineering councils and started faithfully attending their events and volunteering on committees. Longo designed and printed a basic brochure that explained her background, expertise and a brief list of past projects. Prospective clients can sign up for her free "Video Tips" newsletter, in which Longo explains the basics of planning for and executing a technical video. Simply learning more about the process helps most potential clients see how some of their projects might be worth documenting, and the variety of uses those videos might have.*

*Longo also figured that landing a couple of government projects would put her on the map. She registered with the procurement arms of several key governmental agencies, such as the Department of Defense, and consequently is regularly notified when government jobs are coming up for bid. Her standing as an expert on the topic of technical videos was further enhanced when she wrote a 30-page article for an engineering encyclopedia on how to structure a video project. She didn't get paid much for the article, but it has become a key marketing tool; she sent copies to everyone on her newsletter mailing list and uses it as a follow-up when pitching new clients.*

*Finally, Longo turned what could have been a marketing drawback into a major marketing advantage. Because she didn't want to invest the money or space in creating her own production studio, she subcontracted for studio space right from the start with the video production division of a major sports league. Instead of hiding the fact that she doesn't have her own studio, she points out that she has all the latest production technology available for every project. The league's film crews occupy their off-season with special video projects, and Longo has cultivated the goodwill of those crews so that they recommend her to corporate clients.*

# Competitors' Strengths and Weaknesses

No doubt, you're already well aware of your direct competitors. You probably look them in the eye at business and professional associations. If you don't know much about their business operations now, make finding out a top priority. Study their ads, brochures and promotional materials. Drive past their location (and if it's a retail business, make some purchases there). Talk to their customers and examine their pricing. What are they doing well (that you can copy) and what are they doing poorly (that you can capitalize on)?

Information you collect from other sources will supplement your first-hand observations. Suppliers you have in common, industry gossip your sales force picks up, and press releases and expert analyses that run in industry magazines and forums can help you form a multi-dimensional picture of your competitors' strengths and weaknesses.

Here are the basics that you need to know about each direct competitor:

- market share, as compared to your own

- how target buyers perceive or judge your competitor's products and services

- your competitor's financial strength, which affects the ability to spend money on advertising, promotion and pricing

- each competitor's ability and speed of innovation for new products and services

There may be a wealth of other facts that you need to know, depending on the type of business you have. For example, if you're in catalog sales, you'll want to know how fast can your competitors fulfill a typical customer's order, what do they charge for shipping and handling, do they have a typically high rate of returns, and how satisfied are their customers with their entire experience with that company?

Every competitor has definitive weaknesses and strengths that may be points of potential advantage for your company and products. In most cases, larger companies cannot make decisions or allocate resources, personnel and materials as fast as a smaller company under changing market conditions. Smaller companies may have to be content with a limited, but profitable, objective of taking what they can from the market before larger competitors catch up later and often on a larger scale.

You'll also need to realistically assess your ability to compete head-on with an entrenched, powerful, savvy competitor with deep pockets and an inexhaustible determination to dominate the market. For instance, many regional potato-chip makers have carved out profitable, solid specialty niches without tackling giants like Frito-Lay on their own turf.

## Cost of Direct Competition

Ultimately, your most important objective as a small business is to survive and make money. Realistically speaking, there may be times when you'll decide, after careful analysis, that the competition in one area is simply too hot. Here are some situations that may indicate that the cost of direct competition is unwise and ineffective:

1. **When you are faced with taking a loss on any marketing program.** Breakeven spending should also be avoided when done in response to competitive programs. When you get into a price war with a direct competitor, not only are both of you losing money, but customers will soon start to expect deep discounts, and value your services accordingly. It's a short mental trip from "What a deal!" to "Is that all it's worth?"

2. **When your direct competitor can outspend you both in money and quality of the offer.** Larger competitors can almost always outspend you whenever you try to match one of their programs. They can spend more money for longer periods and increase the depth and quality of their discounts and promotional programs.

3. **When your competitor's resources are significantly larger and more effective.** It may make little difference if one of your direct competitors has eight sales people and you have six sales people covering the same geographic area and accounts. However, if your competitors can deliver programs faster on a broader front and still not commit all their forces, you are significantly outgunned. No battlefield general or business manager should risk a head-on confrontation.

4. **When your competitor has more strategic and tactical advantages.** Equal competitive resources may still be strategically and tactically more advantageous than your company's resources. For example, a competitor who spends the same amount in the same media but has an advertising slogan that people love and that becomes a cultural icon ("Where's the Beef?" "Fly the Friendly Skies" "Not Your Father's Oldsmobile") has a strategic advantage. Likewise, a competitor who has strong distributors in all your company's markets, while your company has a few weak distributors in the same markets, has a tactical advantage.

## Case Study — Propaganda, Inc.

*Even when a competitor seems to have a deadlock on a market category, you still may be able to develop a crucial edge. Keith Walton and David Tyreman found a wedge into an apparently already-overcrowded market by interviewing potential customers who weren't giving them business.*

*English transplants to California, Walton and Tyreman were casting about for a business concept so they could quit their corporate jobs as property managers. Antique buffs, they started scouting out, buying, cleaning and selling antiques that small retail stores could use for window and interior retail displays. Old suitcases, picture frames, lace doilies, vases, umbrellas and literally truckloads of similar goods were crowding out their home-turned-warehouse.*

*Still, the partners of Propaganda couldn't understand why they kept getting turned down for projects with big retail chains. When they called on the merchandising managers of major chains, the typical response was "no, we use the X Company." "We thought these people had the market sewn up," says Tyreman. "I had the image of this competitor who was doing everything perfectly. We kept plugging away, but my confidence wasn't high. They had a 50,000 square foot warehouse and we were in a ranch house. I thought, how do we compete with that?"*

*Tyreman finally wangled an appointment with a Macy's executive and went in hoping for a $5,000 order. Instead, he waltzed out with one eight times bigger. Once the project was successfully completed, Tyreman took the executive out to lunch to pick her brain. The first thing he asked her was why she gave Propaganda a chance. As it turned out, he'd made his sales pitch just when Company X had let down the executive for what turned out to be the last time. As she complained about his competitor's sloppiness, late deliveries, insolent attitude about returns, and slothful customer service, Tyreman realized that she probably had plenty of company.*

*"After that, we realized, of course we can compete! We can compete because we really care. So we started phoning (accounts that had previously rejected them) and telling them we were a supplier to Macy's. One reference was all it took." Apparently so—Propaganda now has 17 employees and grosses $3.5 million annually.*

# What Will Your Competitors Do Next?

Once you know the identity of your most direct competitors and have conducted similar research on your secondary competitors, and have sized up your tertiary competitors, too, turn your attention to market trends for each of these sets of competitors. You'll want to speculate not only what your competitors will be reacting to, but what assertive action they'll take, such as introducing groundbreaking products. Knowing all this will help you plan your own strategy effectively. You'll be better able to forecast your own sales, spending and profits; allot the right amounts to advertising and promotion; pace your introduction of new products; and start long-term efforts to outflank your competition as the market evolves.

Getting, and acting on, this competitive intelligence can make the difference between realizing your company's annual plan and losing business that may never be recouped.

To be successful in identifying competitor's strategies and tactics, you must gather every bit of available data from sales forces, outside consultants, market surveys, and trade associations. Collect data on pricing, promotion and advertising spending, new product introductions, sales results, market share trends, packaging innovations, key account management, service levels, and other indicators of competitive activity in the marketplace.

It won't be long before you notice patterns for each key competitor. Some will be very selective, going for well-heeled customers that can afford top dollar. Others may be motivated by gaining the lion's share of the market. Yet others may try to make their mark by being the first to introduce innovations or break into completely new markets. When you understand what your competitors are up to, you'll be able to outflank them by concentrating on market segments they're ignoring, coming up with better ways to deliver your services and products, and even by ceding some territory to them, the better to beat them elsewhere.

## Work Smart

*Here are some useful tactics for gathering competitive intelligence:*

- *Regularly visit your direct competitors' stores, web sites and trade show booths.*

- *Remind your sales force to always be on the lookout for useful bits of information. They can politely ask about a competitor's sales pitch when they're talking with a potential customer. Create a way for this information to get back to you—perhaps through a uniquely flagged e-mail or a special bulletin board on your company's Intranet.*

- *Ask mutual suppliers and customers how things are going for your competitors. Often, suppliers in particular will spill the beans on when a competitor is having a cash crunch, ordering raw materials like gangbusters, or having a tough time getting a new product to market.*

- *Analyze your competitor's products regularly for improvements, weaknesses and quality trends. Mine the required annual and quarterly reports of publicly held competitors for their sales trends, how they're reading the market, and what new products they've got in the pipeline. (You can look up their informative 10-K and 10-Q filings at http://www.sec.gov.)*

- *Call up and ask. Customer service representatives strive (or are supposed to) to give customers complete information and may divulge insider viewpoints if you simply say you have a few questions about how a new product works or a similar inquiry. Pay for a credit report from Dun & Bradstreet or Standard & Poor if knowing your direct competitor's financial trouble (as indicated by delinquent accounts) will give you a market opening.*

- *Bookmark the web sites of key industry research firms and regularly check their press releases to see what projections they're making.*

- *Constantly monitor trade and professional magazines, lists of speakers at conferences, and press releases sent out over news wires.*

- *Subscribe to a customized online news service that will deliver to your e-mail box stories on industry trends and particular competitors.*

- *Make a short list of possible competitive strategies and tactics for the current year, and your retaliatory strategies and tactics, including situations to which you will not respond.*

## Competitive Spending Trends

Competitive spending trends may or may not be a significant influence on your company's budget for supporting products and services. However, in a market where there are one or more large competitors, the amount of money your competitors are willing to spend will affect:

- the success of your current products and services

- your ability to obtain target buyers' attention and purchases

- key accounts' attention and commitment to your programs

- your company's introduction of new products

You'll need to decide how much to spend on proprietary, or custom, research that's highly confidential; buying copies of reports sold by large research firms (usually for several hundred dollars each); and subscribing to specialized and general magazines and news services.

## BUYER IDENTIFICATION AND BEHAVIOR

Who are your buyers, and why do they want your products or services? Are you sure you understand why they choose you over your competitors? To be sure, price and availability of your company's offerings are key factors. However, buyers also choose according to other influences, including their personal, or corporate, culture; demographics; lifestyle; and their personal wants and needs.

When your target buyer is also the end user of your products and services, then you can directly research the demographics, lifestyle and motivations of your buyers.

However, you may be selling to an **intermediate purchaser**— someone who's buying something that will be used by someone else.

In most companies, an information services manager leads a team of technology experts and end users to choose a new software package. Even selling a simple package of paper clips may be a complicated process if a corporate purchasing agent has a long list of specifications as to color, size, volume and the number of paper clips allotted to each department according to its past usage of paper clips and annual budget. Similarly, most retail chains employ buyers who interpret customers' needs and wants, and make huge purchases of goods accordingly.

# Intermediate Purchasers

If you sell to other businesses that turn around and resell your products and services, or are buying on behalf of internal customers, your buyers are predominantly intermediate purchasers. Generally, they fall into three subcategories.

## Business-To-Business or Government Buyers

These types of buyers are subject to much different influences than buyers of consumer goods:

- fewer buyers

- larger business transactions

- regional concentration of buyers

- defined sales and broker relationships

- dependent upon end-user buying patterns and demand

- an inelastic market, meaning that the demand for goods and services is not significantly affected by a significant change in price

Business buyers also take many other factors into account when contemplating buying decisions:

- macroeconomic trends, nationally and internationally

- long-term material supply trends and inventory needs

- delivery rates, timing and reliability

- plant capacities

- suppliers' financial resources

## Consumer-Goods Buyers

These kinds of buyers are subject to different influences when compared with business-to-business or government buyers:

- there may be many buyers at multiple levels in the same company

- the size of the purchase runs the gamut from very small to very large

- national, regional and local buyer concentration

- direct company sales to buyers, or broker relationships

- directly dependent upon end-user buying patterns

- end users are influenced by company advertising and promotion spending

- an elastic market, meaning that the demand for goods and services is easily affected by slight changes in price.

Few intermediate buyers are lone rangers. Usually, they are reporting to a whole chorus of managers, including buying committees, consultants, store managers, franchisees and top management. Intermediate purchasers often collect feedback on new items or lines from layers of managers and end users. Intermediate purchasers have to juggle lots of considerations, including:

- **Profitability of the item** — The higher the margin and dollar profit per item compared to competitive category products, the more likely the corporate buyer will accept it, assuming that price is a driving factor for the ultimate consumer.

- **Discount deals** — When buyers can cut a deal with you, they can charge customers less and push through higher volumes of goods. Discounts on goods to be consumed by employees of a corporate customer directly benefit the company's profits.

- **Advertising and promotion support programs** — Multimedia TV, radio, print and PR support, plus heavy consumer couponing, sweepstakes and contests, are typical consumer packaged goods programs that may be run one to four times a year. Retailers like these because they draw consumers into their stores.

- **Other cash deals** — For example, new item "Slotting Fees" are the subject of controversy and frustration for many manufacturers supplying grocery, drug and mass merchandiser retailers. Slotting fees are cash payments and/or free goods that are not refundable, even if the retailer drops the products after six months. Slotting fees range from a few hundred dollars to over $25,000 per item in some chains.

- **Free goods** — It's common in some retail categories to throw in a free case with an initial order for a new item.

- **Personal buyer/seller relationships** — Personal relationships will always influence buying decisions as long as there are people selling to people. That's why you hire good salespeople!

- **Sales incentive programs** — These programs may spur salespeople on to greater productivity and sales of a particular item or offering.

- **Corporate culture** — Some large companies and governmental agencies have targets for subcontracting to minority and female-owned small businesses.

- **Ease of use** — Technological tools, from internal phone systems to order-taking systems, that are self-explanatory and require minimal training are appealing to corporations that must get many users up to speed on the new tools.

- **Product support and back-up** — Suppliers that quickly and competently fix problems usually get repeat business.

## Case Study — Star Nail, Inc.

*Disposable slippers hardly seem like a growth market, but don't tell that to Tony Cuccio. President of Star Nail, a California manufacturer and distributor of supplies to beauty salons and spas, Cuccio is constantly on the lookout for unaddressed market niches.*

*Star Nail's customers are intermediate purchasers—salon owners who buy quantities of supplies that are either sold directly to consumers or used in the process of giving the customers pedicures, manicures, facials and other services. Often, the products are sent home with the customers who used them, in the hopes that the customer will return to the spa to buy more nail files or other personal care gadgets, for home use.*

*Cuccio was brainstorming with a wholesaler when the two realized that there was an overlooked opportunity in the pedicure category. Salon patrons have to wait as long as 15 minutes for their freshly buffed and painted feet to dry—and that means that they're tying up that pedicure station for 15 long minutes—coincidentally the amount of time that it takes to complete a pedicure right up to the drying stage.*

*Cuccio and the distributor figured that salon owners would scoop up disposable flip-flops that customers could wear around the salon, or even home, as their pedicures dried. They'd be able to fit in as many as a dozen new customers a day for each pedicure station. And customers wouldn't have to hang around the salon, though the flip-flops had to be cheap so that customers wouldn't balk at paying for them.*

*Within weeks, Cuccio had designed a simple prototype from thin foam that wholesaled for less than $1 a pair. He commissioned his Hong Kong supplier to make the flip-flops in a rainbow of bright colors, slid them into simple plastic bags with cardboard tags, and proceeded to sell 1.5 million pairs in the next 10 months.*

*Now, Cuccio is marketing the slippers to health clubs, hotels, resorts, hospitals and other sites where people don't want to walk around in their bare feet through public spaces, but also aren't likely to have their own sandals or flip-flops with them.*

# End Users

If your customers are primarily the ultimate consumers or end users of your product or service, you can build profiles of your most common customer types based on demographics and lifestyle preferences.

Demographics are identifiable, measurable facts that distinguish one group of people from another:

- ethnic background
- age
- income
- education
- sex

- location
- occupation
- number of people/family
- children's ages

Lifestyle analysis is more concerned with the intangibles:

- cultural background
- religious beliefs
- political beliefs
- value systems
- personal fitness and health goals
- recreation and hobbies

- music preferences
- literature preferences
- food preferences/ menu planning
- restaurant preferences
- entertainment preferences
- travel preferences

- level of technological comfort

- social interaction patterns

- social aspirations

- media habits

For instance, it's not easy to identify heavy coffee drinkers just through demographic information. Students and executives alike frequent trendy coffee bars. However, lifestyle analysis indicates several customer profiles, with sets of customers who share similar music, media, recreational and other attributes. When you know the mindset of your customers' lifestyle habits, you can shape the tone of your advertising and promotions to appeal to them effectively.

In some product categories, you'll find several distinct segments with little in common except for their fondness for the product. In the alcoholic beverage market for instance, two such segments are:

- an 18-to-30 age group, primarily male heavy beer drinkers, with sub-segments differentiated by choices of country and western music, rock music, contemporary/jazz and sports interests

- a 39-to-55 age group including both males and females, with an urban skew and sub-segments with wine and hard liquor, differentiated by classical, jazz, new age and soft rock music, with interests in reading, movies, heavy video rentals, more expensive vacations, and both younger and older children

If you're selling directly to your end users, you can collect feedback from them all the time. Train everyone in your company to chat with customers about why they're buying what they are, and from you. Complaints are especially instructive, as a consumer annoyed enough to make a fuss probably has pointed recommendations about how you can improve your product or service.

# THE MARKETING ENVIRONMENT

No company is an island. Even if you're in a specialized market in a small town, you're affected by national and global economic and marketing trends. To be fully prepared, you need to be constantly scanning the horizon for signs of changes that will impact how you do business, and with whom. Look for:

- cultural influences

- governmental and political influences

- demographic and lifestyle trends

- local, national and world economic trends

- the strengths of multi-national competitors

- the influence of technology on the pricing, distribution and positioning of your products and services

Local, state, and federal trade organizations are often the best sources of information on the trends that are likely to influence your business. The federal Department of Commerce (www.doc.gov) offers a wide menu of economic indicators, key statistics and other broad trends. Many states and regions have similar departments of economic development. The Small Business Administration's Small Business Development Centers (SBDCs), mainly located in local community colleges and economic development organizations around the country, offer loads of free assistance with market research (www.sba.com). Don't forget to monitor the web sites of any governmental agency or bureau that regulates your business.

---

### Work Smart

*Research isn't any good unless you use it. Here are some tips for translating your hard-won market intelligence into action:*

- *Organize a way for employees to share and disseminate reports, insights and other intelligence. Circulating printed material is a start, but be sure you complete the loop by including specific questions about how you'll use the information in strategic planning sessions.*

- *Format benchmarking forms so that you can easily plug in information about pricing, customer service and other data for quick comparisons.*

- *Create an "early warning" designation that flags developments that all managers need to know about—and collect their ideas on how to respond.*

- *Foster a corporate culture that includes all employees, including trusted outsourcers, in the process of evaluating your market position.*

- *Tell employees why your market strategy, goals and actions are the way they are. If they understand what you're trying to accomplish, they'll know relevant data when they see it, and can report it back to you.*

---

## FUTURE MARKET GROWTH

How big is your market? Is it large enough to sustain your business and competition? What is the growth trend for the next five years? Once a market has been identified, how can you divide it into bite-sized pieces that you can actually compete in?

As you're tracking market trends, chart changes in the:

- size of the total market

- size of the market interested in your products

- size of the market available for distribution of your products

- size of the market already buying competitive products

- size of the market your company can serve

- size of the market your company can reach with advertising and distribution

For example, the *total potential market* for water purification and filtering devices is 100 percent of the world's population, almost six billion people, since everyone needs to drink pure water. But the size of the *market interested* in water purification devices may be three billion people. The size of the *market available for distribution* may constitute two billion people. But the size of the *market that currently buys* such products may be under 700 million people.

Assume your company is planning to introduce new water purification devices only in the United States and only in the outdoor/camping industry for portable water purification devices. Then the total *market you can serve* for your company's products may be only one million potential users, or 0.02 percent of the total potential world market.

Don't overestimate the size of the market segment that your company can afford to reach with advertising and then distribution. Depending upon your company's resources and size, you may be able to effectively reach only 50 percent of the one million American camping enthusiasts through distributors who are willing to take on your product line. Assuming you are able to afford a modest print magazine ad campaign in two or three national industry magazines, perhaps 50 percent of consumers may be aware of your products, or a net 250,000 potentially interested, aware consumers.

If only one in four interested, aware, available and servable consumers end up buying your product, you have potential sales of 62,500 units/year. Not bad, you say. But if the repeat purchase rate is five years, you would need to generate an entirely new group of 62,500 qualified consumers each year, at least for the first five years. And this may be more difficult to execute than previously thought with a total potential market of almost five billion souls! Perhaps you could increase the distribution base, increase advertising, or increase the served market to include other countries, or expand the product line by creating different sizes of portable water purification devices, or different units for varying severity of non-potable water conditions.

Once you've lined up your best sources of market research and are in the groove of constantly collecting, analyzing and sharing information within your company, it'll become second nature.

# Chapter 3

# Finding Your Target Market

What you don't know can more than hurt you. It can put you out of business. By using your analysis of your market environment, you'll be able to create marketing plan that not only provides a clear direction for your efforts and spending, but will also keep you in constant touch with your customers and clients.

You can know lots *about* your market without knowing what to *do* with that information. As you worked your way through Chapter 2, you may have felt overwhelmed by the breadth and depth of information that you need to collect to get a 360-degree view of your market. Don't despair—gathering market intelligence paves the way for developing a sharply focused plan. And the process of creating the plan will no doubt help you gain momentum for implementing it.

Huge corporations pour billions of dollars annually into unearthing marketing minutiae—how much peanut butter do we eat? Do most people fold or crumple toilet paper? Are we more likely to buy online at certain times of day? Such factoids can be fascinating on their own, but it's what you do with them that converts them into valuable insights. You may not have the time or money to study your market in excruciating detail, but you definitely need to know where, when and how people buy which of your products or services—and most importantly, why.

**What do you need to know, and why?** Your first step is to diagnose your areas of ignorance. If you're already familiar with your market, you've got some insights as to why people buy, but please don't assume that what you've casually observed is the sum total of all your potential customers' motivations. By filling in areas where you're lacking knowledge, you'll be putting in place the crucial building blocks for your marketing plan.

If you're quite vague on the process that your target buyers will go through when they're pondering a purchase from you, you'll want to talk with some actual buyers to find out how they make up their minds about products such as yours. On the other hand, if you're already intimately familiar with your market—say, if you've been selling to these people as a sales rep for a big company and you're now on your own developing a related product within the same target market—you may need only to confirm your direction by monitoring industry trends as reported by news wires, trade associations, independent consultants and similar sources.

Of course, you don't know what you don't know until you take some time to figure out where your blind spots are. Here's a worksheet to help you see where you might be misunderstanding, or not understanding, your target buyer. If you have target buyers in several industries or product categories, complete this exercise for each industry. Your goal for this exercise is to formulate a list of key **benefits** that customers will reap by purchasing your product or service.

---

### Worksheet: HOW WILL YOUR CUSTOMERS BENEFIT FROM PURCHASING YOUR PRODUCTS OR SERVICES?

*What is the primary identity of your target buyer (job title or function)?* _____
_____
_____

*What problem does your target buyer expect to solve (or what aspiration or goal does your buyer hope to achieve) by buying your product or service?* _____
_____
_____

*How does your product or service solve that problem (or help the buyer achieve that aspiration or goal)?* _____
_____
_____

*What other means might your target buyer use to solve the problem (or achieve the aspiration)?*
_____
_____

*Why is it important to your target buyer that this problem be solved (or aspiration achieved)?* ___
_____
_____

---

*How does your target buyer define success with your product (or what is the desired outcome that will satisfy your buyer emotionally and socially as well as functionally)?* _____

_____

_____

*Where and how would your target buyer expect to find out about your product or service?* _____

_____

_____

*What aspect of your product or service (unique positioning statement) do you think will appeal most to your target buyer?* _____

_____

_____

*What core demographic characteristics (age, income, race, family situation, education, career, hobbies, lifestyle preferences, etc.) do your target buyers share in common? For business-to-business products, consider: Do your target customers share a common place in the business cycle (startup or mature) or some other unique characteristic (companies with 20 or fewer employees, companies in a certain geographical area, etc.)* _____

_____

_____

Did you come up empty-handed for some categories? Did you guess on others? If so, you'll need to complete some market research about your customers so that you can effectively develop your product or service to fit their needs—and market it in such a way that they'll know what they'll get from it. (After all, the title of this book describes the benefits that we hope you'll get from reading it!)

**Market research procedures.** Generally, market research procedures break down into primary research and secondary research.

- **Secondary research** — Most of us are familiar with secondary research from doing library research with books and periodicals. With secondary research, someone else has done the actual data gathering in the field and has written it up in a form that's easier for you to use. Secondary research is generally much less time-consuming and cheaper than primary research. However, you're also getting information filtered through the perspective of the researcher. You don't know what that person edited out.

- **Primary research** — This research involves actual data-gathering about the specific usage patterns, product feature likes and dislikes, and so on of target buyers or current users of your products. You gather this data through direct contact with your customers, be it face-to-face, over the phone, or through a mail or online survey.

You could spend a lot of time and money in gathering information on your target market. Before you dive in:

- Prioritize your list of research projects according to how much useful information you're likely to get for the time and cost investment in each source. Set interim deadlines and an overall budget.

- Find out how much it would cost to hire market research specialists to define research problems and design the research. You may be able to be work with a local graduate school of business to be a case study for a class, in which you'd get lots of fresh information for the price of introducing the students to your business and revealing your operations and goals to them.

- Accept the possibility that your limited budget, relatively small amount of original research and not-perfectly-scientific manner of researching may result in some results that are a bit off-target.

## Work Smart

 *Learn how to find what you need from your local public librarian; not only can this person direct you to the right resources within the library, but by paying attention to precisely how the librarian narrows down the search, you'll also learn how you can efficiently unearth information via the Internet.*

*First, compile a list of facts you're trying to research; let's say you've invented a device that senior citizens can use to lift their luggage easily into car trunks. You'll want to find out how many Americans will be in the 65-to-75 age category in the next decade; what companies make travel accessories geared to this age group; and what trade and general publications are worth reading regularly to understand senior citizens' attitudes and abilities regarding domestic travel. Publicly available demographic data compiled by the Census Bureau is in print form at nearly all public libraries and online at www.census.gov.*

*You might scan several copies of* American Demographics *magazine to determine if it addresses your concerns frequently enough to warrant subscribing or at least regularly visiting its web site.*

*Then, find out how other travel product marketers view the needs of senior citizens on the road, and the ability and inclination of seniors to buy specialized travel products. At the same time, gather information on what products in this category exist that might complement and compete with your luggage lifter. Scan travel publications and marketing reports. Contact trade and professional associations and companies that regularly organize trade shows and conferences on your topic.*

*Once you've found some reliable sources in the print world, supplement them by searching online for market reports, competitors' web sites and news sources that you can regularly tap for updates. Many print publications and associations have web sites that are regularly updated with industry news and research reports.*

# SECONDARY MARKET RESEARCH

Secondary research is something every student has completed at one time or another, usually by doing library research with books and periodicals for a school report. This is usually the cheapest and easiest type of research for small businesses to conduct. However, it may be less reliable than primary research because the information you obtain was not developed with your particular problem or situation in mind.

Nevertheless, for some types of information (for example, questions about your competitor's market share or the absolute numbers of potential customers for a new product), secondary market research is the only kind available.

External research involves examining data gathered by industry experts, trade associations, or companies that specialize in gathering and compiling data about various industries.

Internal research is data gathered by your company for purposes other than market research, such as sales reports broken down by product line, that you can use to gauge what the market will do in the future.

## External Secondary Market Research

All businesses, large or small, need to know key information about their marketing environment, competitors and target buyers. Smaller businesses may not be able to afford to subscribe to reports sold by huge national research firms like ACNielsen Corporation (www.acnielsen.com) or Information Resources, Inc., (www.infores.com) because they cost thousands of dollars monthly. Never mind. You can get solid research about total market size, major competitors by category, and target buyers free from industry publications, trade associations, and state and federal commerce departments.

It's relatively easy to track down from outside sources:

- trade association data

- industry publications and databases

- government databases (Census Bureau, state trade measurements, economic indicators)

- Broad industry trends and forecasts from research companies that distribute press releases and charts through news services and their own web sites; one example is Forrester Research (www.forrester.com), which predicts electronic commerce trends

- Omnibus research portals, channels and sites on the Internet aggregate specific types of research by industry and business need. Here are some places to start: InfoSeek (www.infoseek.com); the Marketing Research Association (www.mra-net.org); the Qualitative Research Consultants Association (www.qrca.org); Roper Center for Public Opinion Research (www.ropercenter.uconn.edu/); USAData (www.usadata.com); ActivMedia (www.activmedia.com); Arbitron (www.arbitron.com); CyberAtlas (www.cyberatlas.com); Gallup (www.gallup.com); and MarketFacts, Inc. (www.marketfacts.com). As well, the American Marketing Association (www.ama.org) includes many resources for small businesses and lists member consulting firms, many of which are small businesses themselves; plus, don't forget to visit the *CCH Business Owner's Toolkit*™ (www.toolkit.cch.com) for helpful information and news specifically geared to small business owners

Even for new businesses, internal company data from competitors may be available by interviewing executives of companies that you won't be competing against directly, but whom your competitors do; attending industry trade shows (often research firms and industry leaders showcase their research and projections at speeches and workshops at trade shows and conventions); and asking the right questions from industry experts. They may be unaffordable as consultants but willing to direct you to free databases that you would not ordinarily know of or have access to. And don't overlook your competitor's suppliers. They can be excellent sources of information to aid your research.

Other free or low-cost external secondary research sources include:

- Trade associations

- Computerized databases such as Lexis/Nexis and the pay-per-article archives of major newspapers and magazines such as *The Wall St. Journal*, *Barron's*, *Fortune*, *Forbes*, *Business Week*, *The New York Times*, *Chicago Tribune*, *Los Angeles Times* and *The Washington Post*. If your market is local, mine the archives of your local newspaper to see what your competitors have done in the past

- Your local Chamber of Commerce or a local chapter of a national trade group may yield a number of experts who are willing to dish out free advice for the cost of lunch or dinner

- Colleges and universities for experts working on your field; don't overlook community colleges, your state university system extension, and trade and business schools

- Industry-specific advertising, promotion and public relations agencies

# Internal Secondary Market Research

Secondary research involving the study of information generated by your own company is internal research. Here we're talking about information that was gathered for purposes other than marketing—for example, it may have been gathered for financial or management purposes. (If it were gathered for strictly marketing purposes, it would be considered primary research, not secondary.) The most commonly available internal company information includes:

- daily, weekly, monthly and annual sales reports, broken down by geographical area, product line, or even product

- accounting information (spending and profitability)

- competitive information gathered by the sales force

If you're in retailing or wholesaling, you have a wealth of information at your disposal if you keep detailed information about your sales, by product and related product lines. You may be able to determine not only the types of products that sell best at various times of the year, but even the colors and sizes that your customers prefer. There are a number of inventory tracking software products on the market that can help you keep track of all this information, not only for financial and tax purposes, but for marketing purposes as well. By cross-examining seemingly related product lines (hammers and nails, for instance), you can see if sales of those products do, in fact, move in sync.

# PRIMARY MARKET RESEARCH

*Primary research* is concerned with the design and implementation of *original* research; that is, data collected from the source—in this case, the actual target buyers. The big advantage of doing primary research is that you can get information on the specific question or problem you need answered, not information that merely applies to your industry or type of business in general.

Primary research is generally divided into two categories: "experimental" research and "non-experimental" research.

# Experimental Research

Experimental research is carefully controlled to isolate just the exact factors, such as price as a buying motivator, that the researcher wants precise information about. The researcher screens out, as much as possible, other factors that might muddy consumers' responses to the question at hand. For example, a group of test subjects (who are consumers meeting certain criteria, such as frequent users of the particular product or service in question) might be shown several television commercials. After each one, the group is asked questions designed to measure the likelihood that they'll purchase the product advertised.

Experimental research is often used by large consumer goods companies to test:

- the effectiveness of new advertising or competitors' advertising

- the effect of various prices on sales of a product

- consumer acceptance of new products in trial and repeat-purchase levels

- the effect of different package designs on sales

Experimental research is further divided into two groups:

- **Laboratory studies** — where virtually all variables are controlled except the one being tested, and testing is generally done on the premises of the research company

- **Field studies** — where testing is done in the real world, often by test-marketing the product in a few locations to see whether consumers will buy it

As a practical matter, most small companies bypass expensive laboratory studies and utilize the real market environment to conduct field studies, at less cost than larger companies.

# Laboratory Studies

Laboratory studies are a type of primary marketing research often used by larger consumer products companies. The downside, for small businesses, is that they cost from $50,000 to over $100,000 per segment—and there can be many segments. On the other hand, these tests have a high degree of reliability and correlation with actual market performance when the test product, pricing and advertising are similar to those actually used in the real market. They can save companies many millions of dollars in potentially wasted marketing spending by showing weaknesses in product, advertising, pricing or other variables prior to real-world marketing.

In a typical laboratory study, potential test respondents are approached at a shopping mall and prescreened for type of products used and brand preference. Then they are exposed to some advertising that's being tested and are given a chance to purchase the brand among a competitive array of other products. Finally, the consumers are given some of the product to take home and use. The researcher then follows up with the test respondents to see whether they used the product, how they liked it, and whether they would or did purchase it again. Laboratory tests are generally based upon a minimum of 100 to 300 test-respondents per location, with the tests completed in a few days at a mall or other location where target respondents tend to cluster.

Small companies can conduct small-base simulated testing with local research services or do their own research by showing target buyers advertising, placing prototype products in homes, and following up with carefully constructed questionnaires. However, even 100 to 300 test respondents may still not be a statistically reliable indication of real-world conditions and responses. Smaller companies and local research services are not likely to have a broad database of test response histories or access to sophisticated mathematical computer modeling software. Thus, field studies are often the method of choice for small businesses that want to test a new business idea.

# Field Studies

Field studies are a type of experimental, primary market research that is more likely to be accessible to small businesses. They are generally real-world tests in a controlled group of stores or in a single city.

Research experts often lament the fact that field study participants may very well not reflect the "typical" user. There are considerable opportunities for bias in local or regional market sites, consumer behavior and habits, and local competitive products.

Still, the best test of a product often is actual market conditions. And for many small companies, a real world test is the only experimental research available—anything else is just too expensive.

Professional marketers also sigh over the difficulty of accurately monitoring test results and then estimating larger market acceptance upon national rollout, precisely because the limited field test may pick up on idiosyncrasies of the market environment, consumers, sales forces, competitors, and trade makeup in each region. However, your small business may have no intention of ever rolling out nationally, so a local field test may be all that you'll ever need.

A single retail store or small city test market can provide significant real-world feedback. Thrifty entrepreneurs may design, test, package, produce initial inventories and test-market a new consumer retail product at a cost of $10,000 or less.

Large national and multi-national companies often spend hundreds of thousands of dollars in market research prior to launching a test market for a single product. A large company may spend over $1 million in a single test market for the first six months. While you may not have the desire or the resources to do such extensive testing, the fact that large companies are willing to invest so much money in this type of research should convince you that a small field test of your business idea is worth the effort, before you commit all your funds to the project.

For more on how you can use field studies to try out new business ideas, consider controlled store testing, in which you make your product available in a single store or limited group of stores; or city or regional test marketing, which tends to be more appropriate for larger businesses.

**Controlled store testing.** This can provide test results that reliably simulate real-market conditions and buyers. These methods can lower the cost of testing, save time, and minimize the chance you'll introduce a product or service on a large scale that's roundly rejected by the market.

Many small businesses cannot afford to hire outside consultants and researchers to provide an extensive product development program. However, even a one-person firm can conduct its own in-house controlled testing or new product testing within selected stores.

Many entrepreneurs have successfully designed and conducted their own controlled test marketing by finding a receptive store owner and placing their products in a single store. You can then refine your products before you expand sales beyond this homegrown test vehicle. Both products and services can be tested in this simple, low-cost format.

## Case Study — Cuddlebugg

*When her son Paul, now a grade-schooler, was a baby, Missourian Nancy Dickey found herself wrestling with the straps of his car seat, which were perpetually at odds with his buntings and snowsuits. Getting Paul safely settled in his car seat was such an annoyance that it kept her awake at night.*

*That turned out to be a blessing in disguise, because one night, noodling on the problem, she got a brainstorm: She bounded out of bed and outlined a pattern for an adjustable baby wrap on a flattened grocery sack. The next day, Dickey sacrificed an old orange flannel moving blanket to the cause and stitched up the thing.*

*It was both ugly and practical—and instantly popular. "When people stopped me and asked me about it, I was embarrassed because I had my baby in something so ugly," says Dickey. "Then I remade it in a navy print polar fleece . . . it was cute and warm and people loved it."*

*Though her ad-hoc "focus group" of other supermarket shoppers was giving her encouraging feedback, Dickey was too smart to run out and buy bolts of fleece and start flinging herself at children's store clothing buyers. She turned instead to the Wal-Mart Innovation Network, in Springfield, Missouri, which provides a forum for aspiring inventors. In several sessions, Dickey reviewed everything from the colors and fabric (which the Wal-Mart experts deemed just fine) to packaging (needed to be snazzier) to the best potential markets.*

*Because it's not immediately obvious how to use the CuddleBugg, as Dickey dubbed the clothing contraption, the Wal-Mart merchandising mavens strongly recommended that she sell it through small children's clothing boutiques, where clerks could demonstrate how the CuddleBugg wraps around a child. Not only do clerks in huge discount stores not have the time to explain the product to customers, but the Wal-Mart advisors even doubted that shoppers would have the patience to wade through a set of detailed directions on the package.*

*Dickey followed their advice, and soon was selling thousands of $30 CuddleBuggs annually throughout Midwest children's boutiques. She has also met with success through high-end children's catalogs, which detail in the product layout the steps that a parent takes to wrap a baby in the cozy comforter.*

For business owners contemplating opening a single new store, providing demonstrations of the new product prototype to potential target consumers or buyers can provide a wealth of qualitative data at low financial risk. This informal research can point companies in the right direction for refinement of product features and benefits prior to committing scarce dollars for expensive moulds and production equipment, hiring sales forces, lining up distribution channels, and investing in technology and production facilities.

**City and regional test markets.** These may provide the most reliable real-world feedback on new product success. However, small companies generally do not conduct formal market research field studies in a controlled group of stores, where panels of stores are matched, and distribution, in-store merchandising and advertising is done for you by the market research company for tens of thousands of dollars per test group of stores.

As your company grows, you may have the funds to adopt more sophisticated regional and national tests, including simulated market tests with target consumers in a controlled situation; controlled market tests with a panel of actual retail stores; and computer market simulation modeling.

# Non-Experimental Research

Non-experimental research is done in the normal course of business, where the environment cannot be as closely controlled as in experimental research. Also, the numerous variables of the business can't be as easily isolated. This research centers on measuring the entirety of a project rather than its separate parts.

Non-experimental research is divided into two categories:

- **Qualitative research** — which seeks to obtain many subjective reactions from a limited number of test subjects. If you were seeking to sell automated security systems to gas station owners, you might ask 20 owners a whole menu of questions, from the convenience of the systems they currently use to how they think customers perceive the presence or absence of visible security cameras.

- **Quantitative research** — which seeks to obtain the reactions of many test subjects to a limited number of questions. You might call 100 gas station owners and ask them how much money they'd be willing to spend monthly for a security system linked to a private security firm.

Non-experimental research is often used by companies to explore such "what-ifs" as:

- buyer responses to new products and product improvements (qualitative)

- buyer evaluation of advertising, packaging and brand positioning (qualitative)

- effect of a 10 percent price increase on buyer purchase intent (quantitative)

- testing of a new formula against a similar competitive formula (quantitative)

# Qualitative Research

Qualitative research is *original company research* (primary) on a topic in the normal course of company business (non-experimental). The goal of qualitative research is to get a feel for the research topic, *not* a numerical, statistically predictable measure.

You might conduct a quantitative survey of randomly chosen target customers to see if they are willing to accept an e-mailed newsletter subscription that includes up to three banner ads per issue, but you'd only understand why customers are, or aren't, willing to accept the ads by interviewing them as they subscribe. Their feelings and opinions on this topic will be shaped by their demographic status, geographic location, level of comfort with technology, lifestyle and perceived value of the newsletter to them. *The results of qualitative research depend on the subject matter, the background of research respondents, and the skill of the researcher.*

---

## Potential Pitfall

*Qualitative research results might not accurately represent the entire market! You may inadvertently stumble upon a group of target buyers whose opinions are strongly influenced by an event or circumstance that you don't know anything about.*

*For instance, a dramatic fire in a neighborhood might spark an increase in interest in smoke detectors. If you canvassed that group of worried neighbors, you might mistake their currently keen interest in smoke detectors as a very good sign for your impending city-wide direct-mail marketing campaign for a line of smoke detectors, when, in actuality, smoke detectors wouldn't be a hot item in neighborhoods where no fires had recently occurred.*

---

**Focus groups and interviews.** Traditionally, qualitative research consists of focus groups and individual interviews. Focus groups can be thought of as "group interviews," where a manageable number of target buyers are brought together, presented with an idea or a prototype product, and asked to discuss their opinions with a moderator and with each other.

You can hire a market research company to locate the focus group members according to criteria you specify, and to conduct the session using a professional moderator, while you watch from behind a one-way mirror. Expect to pay $30 to $100 per participant per one- to two-hour session (plus all the coffee they can drink). Usually, groups that are discussing business products or services are paid more than groups discussing consumer products. The total cost of a single focus group, including site, facilitator and follow-up evaluation, may cost upwards of $6,000.

---

## Potential Pitfall

*It's tempting to simply organize a group of friends, colleagues and neighbors into an ersatz focus group. If you do, you may not get honest appraisals of your product or service from the group. After all, they attended the meeting because of their relationship with you; they don't want to hurt your feelings or have their painfully honest comments backfire on their friendship with you. As well, you, as the entrepreneur developing the product or service, may not be able to formulate objective questions that will elicit critical—and helpful—answers.*

*If you're on a tight budget, consider working with a small business development group, local school of business, or industry group to arrange an informal panel of people you don't already know.*

You can also conduct your own individual interviews with potential target buyers or with people who already purchase a competitive product. If you've already determined that the market is large enough to support your product, have a prototype made up and ask people to evaluate it using a short questionnaire.

As you're experimenting with various types of qualitative research, you'll soon develop a sixth sense for what types of research yield the most helpful feedback. Don't forget—big companies pay big bucks to listen as closely to their target buyers as you can every day. That's a strategic advantage right there.

**Qualitative questionnaires.** To get an accurate handle on what the market's reaction will be, at least 25 qualified people should be interviewed for each significant product difference. This will give you a sufficient frame of reference for adjusting the actual product or service, or how you position it compared to the competition.

For smaller companies, selecting interviewees from local surroundings (e.g., local neighborhood for a single retail store) may be the most practical alternative. As your company grows, you'll want to obtain as representative a sample of interviewees as possible throughout your ever-expanding marketing area.

The problem with qualitative research is that you must take it with a grain of salt. The smaller the number of people you survey, the less likely it is that their opinions represent those of your entire target market. If 100 percent of qualitative test respondents like your new product, perhaps it has significant merit. On the other hand, perhaps one "loudmouth" in the focus group liked it, and everyone else was afraid to voice a contrary opinion.

That's why it's so important to find out additional characteristics of the people you're surveying. The questionnaire for qualitative research might collect:

- demographic information (their age, sex, occupation, home locale, income range, occupation, number and age of children, and other relevant vital statistics)

- confirmation that they use the product or service you're testing, or would, if an attractive alternative was presented to them

- which brands they currently purchase or use

- how often they buy those brands

- why they like different brands

- what they disliked about different brands

- a discussion of different product attributes and benefits

- a discussion of the importance of various product attributes and benefits

- an evaluation of product prototype

Ideally, your test results should be confirmed by quantitative research or a real-market field test.

# Quantitative Research

Quantitative research is a type of non-experimental market research that provides numerical measurement and reliable statistical predictability of the results to the total target population. Like qualitative research, this is original company research (primary) on a subject in the normal course of company business (non-experimental).

Quantitative research is distinguished from qualitative research primarily by the large numbers of people who are questioned (sampled respondents) and the type of questions asked. Generally, sample sizes of 100 are adequate for simple "yes/no" questions to get results that are 95 percent reliable as being accurate for the entire market of buyers. To increase the accuracy to 97 percent to 99 percent, the sample sizes would have to increase to 400-2,000 or more, depending upon the subject matter and complexity of questioning.

For example, you might design a prototype product that you evaluate using qualitative research through a focus group comprised of target consumers. Once the features and benefits of the prototype have been refined according to the feedback you got from those potential consumers, and you've gathered their thoughts on how to position the product or service, you may want to also launch a quantitative test.

At this point, larger companies continue to refine the prototypes and may conduct a series of blind tests, in-home usage studies, and even market forecast simulations costing up to $100,000. For smaller companies, it may be less expensive, faster and just as accurate to do a small field-study test in the real market, despite the risks that the results of the test may not translate to other markets.

To do good quantitative research, you need the following three elements: a well-designed questionnaire, a randomly selected sample and a sufficiently large sample.

**Quantitative questionnaires.** The design of a good quantitative questionnaire depends upon careful consideration of:

- What decisions are going to be based upon the test results?

- What key information do you need to make these decisions?

- What information was gathered in qualitative research that would be useful?

- How should test respondents be screened for demographic and lifestyle backgrounds?

- How many respondents are necessary for statistical reliability for different questions?

- How will you tabulate and analyze questionnaire results?

Questions may be posed in writing, by fax or over the phone, but generally phone interviews have a better response rate. If you use the phone, you will want the telemarketer to use a script, to be sure that each respondent is answering the same questions. It's best to hire a telemarketing firm with professional survey takers who can keep the respondents on track and on topic.

Quantitative questionnaires are similar to qualitative questionnaires, but usually gather more information that can be numerically tabulated with significant statistical predictability. Questions should be based upon common sense and good communication practices. All questions should be directly related to providing useful information for decision-making; the survey company you hire to manage the project can help you phrase questions so they're easily understood, but don't beg certain answers. (Leading the respondents to particular conclusions will undoubtedly result in skewed information.)

For example, a questionnaire could include:

- demographic information (age, sex, occupation, home locale, income range and other vital statistics)

- confirmation that the respondent uses the product or service you're testing

- which brands are used or purchased

- how often brands are purchased

- why the respondent likes different brands

- what he or she dislikes about brands

- the importance of different brand images

- a ranking of brands by preference

- whether price makes a difference to the frequency of purchasing different brands

- evaluation of different product attributes

- ranking of product attributes' and benefits' importance for buyers

- evaluation of brand positionings and advertising

- purchase intent on a five-point scale (definitely, maybe, indifferent, maybe not, definitely not)

- brands that would be replaced by your new product or service

Construct questions that allow test respondents to easily understand and answer them. Questions should be ones that your targeted test respondents will most likely know the answers to and would be willing to provide information on. Avoid:

- vague questions

- irrelevant background questions

- trick questions

- questions outside the expected knowledge and experience base of respondents

## Work Smart

*Small companies often provide simple questionnaires to customers when they come into the store or purchase products and services. They may use the questionnaires to obtain a qualitative pulse, or check, mainly to verify that nothing is going terribly wrong in their day-to-day operations. Or they may use the questionnaires to measure the effectiveness of local advertising media in generating store traffic.*

*You can also capture the customers' names and addresses to build a mailing list for promotions and advertising. And you can let customers opt into a pool of focus group candidates simply by providing a "Yes, I'd be willing to tell you more!" box to check.*

*Over time, you may obtain results that are almost as good as quantitative test results, particularly if you ask simple "yes/no" questions (on customer satisfaction, for example). Be sure to provide a slotted box with a lock on it so customers are assured that their responses are confidential to management.*

**Sample selection.** There are two ways to select test respondents:

- probability samples (randomly selected samples)

- non-probability samples

With probability sampling, each test respondent sampled has an equal chance of being selected for testing. This means that test results have a better chance of being representative of the entire target population.

For example, if we were to test how many America Online members use a particular software package, we could theoretically obtain a list from AOL and randomly sample 400 members by mail, phone or e-mail to obtain a representative probability sample. (In reality, AOL does not release this information.)

If we were to try to sample 400 AOL members outside a given computer store for our survey, it would be a non-probability sample. The group of people we approach may be biased by including too many students, businessmen, single vs. married people, bargain hunters or some other category of consumer, depending on the location of the store, day of the week, time of day and what attracted people to the store that day.

Many small companies utilize only non-probability sampling methods in their research. This may be due to budget constraints or just because they're comfortable with that method of researching target customers. Beware, though: The differences in results from probability and non-probability methods can be significant. Only probability sampling provides a true representation of the total target population, accurate predictability and distribution levels.

Non-probability sampling has built-in biases that cannot be separated or measured. If a high degree of accuracy and predictability is *not* required, as in early exploratory stages of new product development, then you might be able to get away with a "convenience" non-probability sampling method. But don't stake your company on it.

**Sample Size and Distribution.** If you're doing quantitative market research, in most cases, the sample size for the number of respondents you'll test is determined by your available budget and by the confidence levels that you desire or can accept.

The larger the sample size, the greater degree of accuracy, not only for predictions of total population behavior, but also for the degree of variation in that behavior.

This is the basis for determining confidence levels in predictability of the test base compared to the entire target population. *The larger the sample size, the smaller the standard error—the possibility that the test results will not mirror the behavior of the target population.* On the other hand, if your sample grows beyond a certain size, you will not greatly increase your accuracy level, but you will definitely incur more research costs.

Even for small companies, the best recommendation for choosing the optimum sample size is to consult a professional market researcher or a nearby school with a statistics department for help in designing the model, constructing questionnaires, conducting the research and analyzing results.

**A statistics primer.** In order to get your money's worth from any quantitative research that you conduct, you need to understand how it works. Here's a crash course in the basics of statistical procedures and evaluation. Don't despair! Common sense lurks behind the methods and numbers.

At least 100 test respondents should be selected from a probability sample for all quantitative tests to get to the level where you can be confident that the results reflect your overall market with a 68 to 95 percent accuracy rate.

When sample sizes are at least 100 and the results are translated to a graph, the results will tend to approximate what is called the normal curve of distribution. That is, the majority of people will give you an "average" response, a smaller number will give you a "below average" or an "above average" response, and a very small number will give you an "exceptionally below average" or an "exceptionally above average" response. This distribution is also known as a bell curve. The mathematical probability that a given test observation will fall within a range of values from the middle of this normal distribution curve is called a standard deviation.

**Standard Deviations**

There is a direct relationship between your sample size and the degree of reliability, based on the statistically predictable behavior of respondents' test results clustering in the pattern of a normal curve. The more people you have in your survey, the more likely that their responses will fall into the classic bell curve. When you've got a group of 100 to 200 randomly chosen people, you can start to be quite—about 95 percent—confident that their responses represent your market as a whole.

# Chapter 4

# Building a Plan To Reach Your Market

As you're collecting and evaluating all these sorts of market research, you can start fitting it into a marketing plan. There's no single formula for marketing plans, so we haven't included a fill-in-the-blank exercise on this. A general plan is outlined at the end of this book on page 202; adapt it to fit your company's objectives. However, all successful marketing plans essentially outline who the market is, what benefits the products or services deliver to that market, at what price, and through what means.

Begin with a simple plan that defines your primary and secondary target markets, what they want and need from your product or service, how much they are willing to pay for it that will still return a reasonable profit to you, and general strategies that you can use to reach them.

## CREATING A MARKETING PLAN

Your primary market is the population that's most likely to want your product, to pay the most for it, and to buy it most frequently. A golf resort mainly positions itself as a haven for golfers. Managers hope to cultivate a loyal following of golfers who will return frequently, preferably with well-heeled friends.

Your product or service will fit the bill often, but not as predictably, for your secondary market. Golf resorts are popular locales for business conferences, partly because many businesspeople are golf aficionados, but also because the resorts usually have spacious facilities for meetings and top-notch food service facilities (and often spas and other athletic facilities for the golf-impaired).

As you compile results from your quantitative research, build a profile of your most likely primary customers. Sift through the information you have to see how much they make, where they live and how they spend their leisure time; or, if you're targeting other businesses, profile those that could use your product or service to fuel their own growth plans, by streamlining operations, delivering desired results more quickly, giving them more options to offer their own customers, and other results.

## Assessing Perceived Benefits

As you're doing this, continually ask yourself: What will my target buyer get by using my product or service? Keep in mind:

- **Direct, immediate benefits** — These are ways that your product or service immediately starts to help the consumer or business achieve the results they want. A new tire provides a direct, immediate benefit to a car owner with a flat.

- **Direct, medium- or long-term benefits** — Many long-term consulting and technological upgrade projects fall into this category. It may take two years to install a new accounting computer software system, and another six months for all your client's operations to be converted to the new system, but the savings through efficiency, better financial planning and control, and better integration with the clients' other computer systems may reverberate for a decade or longer.

- **Indirect benefits** — The process of planning and installing that new accounting system may entail revamping the way work and money flow through your client's accounts receivable and accounts payable departments. While that revamping paves the way for the new accounting system, it also has value of its own. Yet, the two departments might not have had the impetus to be revamped otherwise; the imminent installation of the new system is a catalyst for the changes. That's an indirect, but welcome, benefit, of preparing for the new accounting system.

- **Specific ways that your product or service delivers these benefits** — Speed, consistency, reliability, top quality, cost effectiveness, inexpensiveness with flair, and accuracy are just a few product attributes that help potential buyers understand the context in which they'll get the product benefits that they're buying.

- **Crucial ways that you are different from your competitors, either in actuality or in your customers' perceptions** — You may not want to slam your competitors by name ("Joe's Market—Cleaner than Sam's!"), but you will definitely want to cultivate positive perceptions that shape your image in the mind of the buying public ("Joe's Market—Fresh Food, Friendly Service, Sparkling Surroundings").

## Potential Pitfall

*It's easy to confuse product attributes with product benefits—but don't.*

*Attributes (sometimes called features) describe what a product is. A personal calendar system may be leather-bound, have seemingly endless time-management categories, and be accompanied by a training session on how to use your time more efficiently.*

*Benefits describe what a product delivers to the customer. The people who buy the personal calendar system don't mainly want to get a leather desk accessory. They want to use their time more effectively and efficiently, learn new ways to set and stick to priorities, get more out of their day, and free up time from work for personal pursuits.*

*An effective marketing campaign for the calendar system might have a theme such as "Get a day for yourself for every hour you spend with us"—a theme that zeros in on what customers will get for their investment in learning and using the system. If the system is that great, who cares if the case is leather or cardboard?*

# Profiling Your Target Markets

Meanwhile, you may also have picked up some not-so-great feedback about your product or service as you've researched your target market. If you uncover an odd result, don't shrug it off. Get a second opinion—perhaps from a consultant or seasoned entrepreneur in a related market—that can help shed some light on the mystery.

Even, perhaps especially, if it seems to confirm your wildest dreams, don't jump to conclusions on the basis of a one overly enthusiastic focus group. Make sure you've got the whole picture by contrasting your qualitative findings and primary research with general industry, consumer and economic trends, and established wisdom about how your target market tends to behave.

Based on your research, create a profile of your primary and secondary target markets.

If you're marketing to consumers, start with:

- age
- gender
- profession/career
- income level

- educational level

- place of residence

- family status

- information specific to your product, such as hobbies; whether they rent or own their home; how many cars, computers, televisions or bathrooms they have; and so on

If you're marketing to another business, begin with:

- Size of business:

  — by number of employees

  — by annual revenue

- Locale of companies:

  — one location or many?

  — concentrated in one geographical area or spread out?

- Growth trends in the target industry:

  — specific products and services your business customers sell

  — how much is your target consumer category or industry projected to spend on your category of products or services in the next year?

  — the next five years?

Next, choose several head-to-head competitors and profile their marketing strategies according to:

- Years in business

- Market share

- Brand image

- Specific product features

- Specific claimed customer benefits

- Pricing strategy (do they frequently discount?)

- List three specific strengths of this competitor

- List three specific weaknesses of this competitor

How does your industry prefer to buy? Is it cliquish, buying only from an old boys' or girls' network? Do purchasing decisions for your product tend to be driven by price or by specific benefits? Which benefits are most compelling?

How does your product or service differ significantly from your competitors?

How will your product or service give your customers an edge over their competitors?

# OUTLINING A MARKETING BUDGET

A successful marketing budget focuses just as much on what you get for your expenditures as how much you're expending. As you consider various media and strategies, ask yourself how you'll evaluate the results. It's smart to spend money only if you have a way to track how much you're getting for it. As you track the success of various campaigns, you can shift resources to those that work best, and kick off an upward cycle of more effective marketing resulting in higher sales, richer profits and more money to spend on yet-more-effective marketing.

Get a grip on how much you'll need to spend by evaluating methods already being used.

## Traditional Marketing Media

How are your customers accustomed to hearing about products and services such as yours?

- Television

- Radio

- Newspapers

- Consumer/lifestyle magazines

- Business/Trade magazines

- Hobby/technical/travel/specialized magazines

- Searching the Internet

- Directly visiting certain web sites (customized news feeds, popular portals and specialty and corporate sites)

- Direct mail or direct e-mail

- Phone calls

- Personal sales visits

- Yellow Pages

- Outdoor signs and billboards

- Signs on your place of business

- Word of mouth/recommendations

- Internet chat rooms, bulletin boards, newsgroups and listservs

- Trade shows

- Conferences

- Promotions

- Sponsorship of special events

## Competitive Marketing Strategies

Next, examine the effectiveness of the marketing campaigns of several leaders in your category. What balance of the above media, and others, do they appear to use? Can you find out more about their marketing plans through their press releases, SEC filings (if they're publicly held) and through shrewd observation? How effective are these advertising, promotional and public relations efforts? Do they appear to be shifting more money and effort from one strategy to another?

Collect media kits (which outline target market demographics, spending patterns, industry trends and buying patterns) from magazines and newspapers that seem to reach your target market. You can also visit those publications' web sites; most have some sort of online media kit. Closely examine the amount charged for ads, radio spots and other media. Don't be afraid to ask media reps how their most successful advertisers track response. Don't worry quite yet about actually buying ad space—we'll get into that in Chapter 9. For now, use the media kits to get an idea as to how much it costs to run ads of various sizes.

## Your Specific Marketing Plan

Now, compare your observations about how your customers like to hear about services and products such as yours, with what media your competitors are using to reach your target customers. How much overlap is there? Might there be an opportunity for you to make a splash with a refreshingly new approach, or do your target customers truly prefer the tried and true?

What are the top three or four media that are both used effectively by your competitors and well received by your target customers?

How might you roughly allot your marketing budget among these categories? For instance, a restaurant might allot 40 percent of its annual budget to local newspaper and magazine advertising, 20 percent to a yellow pages ad, 35 percent on a web site that features an online ordering option, and the remaining 5 percent to pay for tracking the effectiveness of all these media. (Don't forget to include the cost of measuring the effectiveness of your marketing efforts.)

As you're organizing all this material, you'll start to see specific patterns emerge. You'll notice what your competitors aren't saying about themselves, which may open up opportunities for you to stake out a distinctive selling point. You'll notice where your competitors are following the crowd and what the maverick is doing. Along the way, you'll develop a sense of where you want to position your products and services, and what kind of image you want to cultivate that will distinguish your company from the pack.

## Worksheet: SHAPING YOUR UNIQUE POSITIONING STATEMENT

I. *Objective—where do you want your company to be in five to ten years?*

    A. *Target market penetration (percentage of market share you want to own)*

    B. *Target corporate revenue*

    C. *Target corporate profits*

II. *Who are your Target Buyers?*

    A. *What problems are they seeking to solve, or aspirations are they seeking to achieve, by purchasing your products and services?*

    B. *How are they currently solving this problem or addressing this aspiration?*

    C. *How is your product or service better than what they're already doing?*

    D. *What are their top concerns in the buying decision? (convenience, price, availability, reliability, uniqueness, durability, ease of use)*

    E. *Which of these priorities does your product or service best address?*

    F. *What is your unique positioning statement?*

III. *Market Scope*

    A. *Who are your primary competitors?*

- *Why are your target buyers currently purchasing from them?*

- *What features do their products offer that yours don't? (and vice versa)*

- *What features do you offer that they don't? (and vice versa)*

- *What other factors (size, marketing budget, location, reputation, ability to quickly adapt to changing market) do they possess that you must take into consideration?*

    B. *Who are your secondary competitors?*

- *What do they offer that appeals to your target buyers?*

- *What market trends do they represent that may change the way your target buyers think about your product category and specific products and services?*

    C. *Who are your tertiary competitors?*

- *What do they offer that appeals to your target buyers?*

- *What market trends do they represent that may change the way your target buyers think about your product category and specific products and services?*

IV. *Reaching and Developing a Relationship with your Target Buyers*

    A. *How are they accustomed to hearing about products in this category?*

    B. *How are they accustomed to learning more about products that interest them?*

    C. *How are they accustomed to actually purchasing products or services such as yours?*

    D. *Do you need to develop a two-step strategy to reach intermediate buyers and target buyers?*

    E. *How much are they accustomed to paying for this type of product or service?*

    F. *How are they accustomed to receiving the product or service?*

    G. *What kind of relationship do they expect to have with the seller of products or services such as yours?*

    H. *How do they define satisfaction with a product or service such as yours?*

    I. *How do you want them to be able to describe their experience with the product or service and your company?*

V. *Corporate and Product or Service Image and Positioning*

    A. *What characteristics do you want your company to be known for?*

    B.   *How do those characteristics benefit your target customers?*

    C.   *What unique characteristics best define your products or services?*

    D.   *How do those characteristics directly benefit your target customers?*

    E.   *What is your company's Unique Positioning Statement?*

VI.  *How is each line or major product that you offer unique and better than your competition?*

    A.   *What does it do?*

    B.   *What does it accomplish for users?*

    C.   *What features/options/elements about it are unique?*

    D.   *What particular advantages does it have over direct competitors?*

    E.   *What is its Unique Positioning Statement?*

## Worksheet: CRAFTING A CORPORATE IMAGE STRATEGY

I.   *Develop long-term (in five years) corporate growth goals for:*

    A.   *Market position*

    B.   *Revenues*

    C.   *Profits*

II.  *Create a corporate unique positioning statement by examining:*

    A.   *What is your current corporate image?*

    B.   *What do you want your company to be known for? (i.e., when your company's name is mentioned, people immediately think of these characteristics)*

    C.   *How do you want target buyers and current customers to hear about your company?*

    D.   *How will marketing for specific products, services, and lines that you offer be consistent with the corporate image you want to build?*

III.  *Devise corporate communications tools that help you build and reinforce the image you seek:*

    A.   *Logo/official graphic style*

    B.   *Written materials (brochures, fliers, media kits, sales kits)*

    C.   *Web site*

    D.   *Presentation materials*

E.  *Signs*

F.  *Advertising style/taglines*

G.  *Promotions*

H.  *Sales force training*

I.  *Customer service training*

J.  *Trade show materials*

K.  *Conference/speaking/professional networking materials*

## Worksheet: CRAFTING A PRODUCT/SERVICE MARKETING STRATEGY

(complete for each primary line, product or service category, or primary product)

I.  *Develop long-term (in five years) product/service growth goals for:*

A.  *Market position*

B.  *Revenues*

C.  *Profits*

II.  *Create a product/service unique positioning statement by examining:*

A.  *What is the current image of your product or service?*

B.  *What do you want this product or service to be known for? (i.e., when the product's or service's name is mentioned, people immediately think of these characteristics)*

C.  *How do you want target buyers and current customers to hear about this product or service?*

D.  *How will marketing for this product or service be consistent with the corporate image you want to build?*

III.  *Find specific marketing channels that will convey the unique benefits of this product or service most effectively:*

A.  *Advertising*

B.  *Media relations*

C.  *Promotions*

D.  *Community relations/promotions*

E.   *Speaking to professional audiences/contributing to professional or industry journals*

F.   *Participation in business and trade groups*

G.   *Unique packaging*

H.   *Unique distribution method*

I.   *Web site with electronic ordering and customer service*

J.   *Direct mail*

K.   *Direct selling (individually or in small groups)*

IV.   *Devise effective support materials that help you build and reinforce the image you seek for the product or service:*

A.   *Logo/official graphic style*

B.   *Written materials (brochures, fliers, media kits, sales kits)*

C.   *Web site*

D.   *Presentation materials*

E.   *Signs*

F.   *Advertising style/taglines*

G.   *Promotions*

H.   *Complementary materials*

I.   *Sales force training*

J.   *Customer service training*

V.   *Measure your strategy's effectiveness:*

A.   *What media and techniques will you use to first introduce a new product or service to target buyers?*

B.   *How will you follow up?*

C.   *What customer service and post-sale customer contact will reinforce the image of the product or service as well as the company image you are cultivating?*

# Part **II**

---

# From Plans to Actions

By now, you've got a firm grip on who your potential customers are, and what they need and want. Now we're going to move into the specifics of how you can shape your products, services, packaging and pricing to meet those expectations.

Internal decisions, such as deciding on how much to charge for your product or service, are often overlooked by businesspeople who think that marketing is comprised of activities that take place in public, such as advertising and community relations. In fact, specific decisions about how to price, present and deliver your products and services send clear, strong messages to customers.

Sales, advertising, promotions, media relation and professional relations are only effective if they reinforce the market position communicated by your pricing and presentation. No element of the marketing plan stands on its own. They all interrelate—hopefully by complementing, not contradicting, each other. Experimentation will help you find the right balance of specific marketing activities that most effectively reach your customers.

Remember The Man Who Marketed Too Much (from page 1)? He had lots of ideas for marketing projects, but no marketing focus. He never bothered to define his unique positioning statement, so he literally didn't know how his little company was positioned in the

---

market, or even if he was offering anything more than just a me-too service. No wonder he went out of business in just months—he was never really *in* business.

You, though, have taken the time to understand the big picture. Now let's examine the specific methods of achieving the marketing goals you've created as you worked your way through Part I.

*Chapter 5: Developing, Refining and Branding Your Product* will help you apply the specific expectations and aspirations of your target market to your product or service, so that what you take to market is what people want.

*Chapter 6: Packaging and Pricing Your Product* provides numerous ways to present and price your product or service so that you're attracting your target customers.

*Chapter 7: Choosing Distribution Methods* outlines the importance of getting your product or service to customers via methods that reinforce your market position.

*Chapter 8: Sales and Customer Relations* arms you to make your case directly to your potential customers—and to keep on serving them well.

*Chapter 9: Promotion and Advertising* will equip you to create and launch promotional and advertising campaigns that will attract the audiences you want with the message that will draw them in.

*Chapter 10: Media, Community and Professional Relations* gets you up-to-speed on these highly effective, but often misunderstood, modes of getting your message to potential customers.

*Chapter 11: Are You Getting What You're Paying For?* outlines ways that you can evaluate the success of your marketing efforts.

The ultimate badge of success, of course, isn't found in just satisfied customers, or repeat customers, or soaring sales, or market dominance. It's in the right balance of all those things—when you're gaining and keeping customers *and* increasing sales and profits—while enjoying the ride.

# Chapter 5

# Developing, Refining and Branding Your Product

New businesses are always in a rush to get new products to market. But how many new products or new businesses fail because the concept is never quite executed correctly for the intended target buyer? When a company doesn't take the time to do it right in the first place, it somehow always has to find the time to correct it later, often at great cost in unnecessary spending, lost time, lost sales, and lost market share—not to mention the embarrassment factor.

The fastest way to go out of business is to introduce a great idea, but to never completely deliver the features or benefits that were promised. People who initially buy and then reject a new product aren't likely to give you another chance. When you include failed brand extensions, the failure rate for new product introductions approaches 80 percent in some categories. That's why testing your concepts is so important.

The classic approach to rolling out new products follows these steps:

- **Company mission** must be developed or confirmed.

- **Product development strategy** must be determined and refined.

- **New product ideas** must be generated.

- **Ideas must be screened** for potential profitability and fit with company goals.

- **New product prototypes** must be developed and refined.

- Packaging, pricing, distribution, and advertising **strategies** must be developed and refined.

- **Success of the new product** must be measured after introduction.

# DEVELOPING A MISSION STATEMENT

A company mission statement can be a powerful force to clearly define your company's purpose for existence. In the beginning, your company was formed to accomplish something that did not exist in the marketplace, or to do a better job than existing companies. What was that special purpose?

*The commitment to formulating a company mission can be critical to your company's success.* It helps keep management focused on preserving or strengthening the company's unique competitive niche, because it defines not only what you do, but also what you don't do. When a competitor suddenly comes out with a splashy new product, your mission statement can help keep you from making panicky knee-jerk responses. It's easy to kick into a reactive mode: "If Jane's music store is launching its own recording studio, then we have to!" That's less of a temptation when you're grounded by a mission statement that is periodically updated to reflect changing market conditions and your evolving corporate growth strategy.

The most successful company missions are measurable, definable, and compelling calls to action. The statement should also include all employees—for example, a statement that only product engineers can help make a reality won't do much to motivate or focus everyone else.

## Work Smart

*Vague aspirations—"to be the paper supplier of choice"—may sound good on paper, but a punchy statement—"delivering the right paper to the right place at the right time"—can be measured every day by every employee. Did that customer get the right paper? At the right place? On time?*

*If the mission statement of our paper distributor was instead to "be the biggest supplier of copier paper to the top 25 percent of corporations in our market," then its marketing strategies would be quite different, possibly calling for alliances with copy machine repair companies and emphasis on volume orders, rather than just-in-time delivery.*

As you continually weigh information from your ongoing market analysis, you may decide to respond to your market in a wholly different way, and thus change your mission statement correspondingly.

# Creating a Workable Company Mission

A "call to action" mission statement provides key attributes that are often missing in other company mission statements:

- it elicits an emotional, motivational response in your employees

- it is easily understood and can be transferred into individual action every day

- it is a measurable, tangible goal

- it is firmly rooted in the competitive environment in which the company operates

A company's mission statement is also influenced by:

- company history and traditions

- management preferences

- distinctive competencies of the company

- company resources

- competitive strengths and weaknesses

Today's accelerated rate of change and information growth means small companies will inevitably face increased competition in their market niches. Small companies need to embrace and seek out change, rather than avoid it or wait until change is forced upon them by competitors.

*You're likely to change slogans as you freshen advertising and promotional campaigns, while your corporate mission statement will change as you shift your strategic market position to take advantage of new opportunities.*

## Cultivating a Brand

Conventional wisdom used to hold that you'd first create a line of products or services, develop a reputation (hopefully, a good one) in the market, then distill the essence of that reputation into a brand.

The problem with that approach is that it assumes that customers will omnisciently detect your overall company strategy as they observe your gradual rollout of products and services. Of course, most of your customers, be they consumers or other businesses, are preoccupied with their own lives and activities, and aren't spending much time speculating on what your next move might be or what your evolving company brand is. When you grandly unveil your official brand, the response is likely to be a collective yawn.

The concept of a brand is still sound: It's the crystallization of the essence of your company, typically represented by a picture (or a logo) that is often accompanied by a phrase. Your company is more than just the sum of its parts—you, your employees, your products, and your equipment and group good attitude. The brand symbolizes the "more than the sum."

You've already got a well defined unique positioning statement, so you've accomplished much of the work of formulating your brand identity. When you consciously cultivate a brand from the beginning, it makes it easier to develop new products and services; instead of launching new efforts and then trying to figure out how they fit into your company direction, your brand is a litmus test against which potential new launches are measured. "What will extend this brand?" is a more helpful question to ask yourself than "What other products might our target market want?" Serving breakfast sandwiches was a perfect fit with the McDonald's brand, which promises quick, convenient, generic, inexpensive food. Launching a chain of white-tablecloth seafood restaurants featuring recipes developed by celebrity chefs would be a radical (and highly unlikely) departure from the established McDonald's brand.

As you shape your brand, ask yourself:

- What do you want people to think of when they think of your company?

- What "tone of voice" do you want to convey to your market?

- What would be your response if a potential customer asked you, "What can I count on from you?"

- What company values differentiate your company in your market?

- How is the company bigger than you and your personal goals for it?

Keep your eye on the end result that you want your customer to reap by choosing your brand over a competitor's similar-seeming product or service. Because the brand exists only in the minds of your customers, what it means depends wholly on what it means to them. You may think that your brand stands for high-quality nails, but a building contractor who has lost time and money replacing boxes of your imperfectly formed nails that jammed up his crew's nail guns will beg to differ. To him, your brand stands for second-rate—at best.

That's why it's so important to continually monitor how your brand is perceived, and how that brand message is contradicted or reinforced by the actual experience your customers have with your company.

Two rival home-grocery delivery services, for instance, initially perceived the same problem: Two-career families and others with more money than time didn't want to hassle with the weekly chore of tromping to and through the local store to buy unexciting commodities like milk, cheese and scouring pads. Each hit on the same solution: A delivery service that offers on-line ordering and top-quality groceries, plucked from local suppliers and delivered to the customer's door at a specified time.

There, the two companies' brands diverged. One realized early on that it could peddle information culled from customer orders to food and household good manufacturers, sell ads on its web site, and push additional home services to current customers. Great ideas—except that the core delivery service suffered as company officials chased after the other sources of revenue. Sporadic efforts to reinforce the brand, which enjoyed an early start compared to its competitors, helped to keep a thin line of customers coming in.

Meanwhile, executives with a rival company steadfastly refused to be diverted from their mission of saving customers time and hassle through home delivery. Company founders thought about how they'd handle the tempting add-ons, and decided before they even took their first order that they wouldn't introduce any additional service that clashed in any way with the core brand philosophy. They did eventually add other home-delivery services, such as video rentals and dry cleaning, because they felt those services underscored the core brand image.

Within a few years, the first company had muddied its mission by redefining it as a marketing information company that also happened to deliver groceries. After ten years, it wasn't making any money. The second company, though, not only had average customer orders six times that of its early-arrival rival, but also became profitable.

What if your brand is yourself? The same principle applies, even if you are one-person accounting shop. If you decide to specialize in estate planning, that means that you aren't pursuing business with small companies. You deliberately cultivate your expertise in estate planning—and so become established in the minds of your clients as a walking encyclopedia of various sorts of wills and the mysteries of probate court. They don't expect you to have a professional opinion on international trade issues—and probably wouldn't want to accept advice from you on that topic, anyway, because they primarily know you as an estate planning accountant.

## Work Smart

*It's important that your brand be consistently portrayed in all your company materials, from employee handbooks to letterhead to print advertisements to web page. Varying the color, type style, and other visual elements on different marketing pieces will confuse customers. That's why it's so important to choose your logo, brand statement, marketing slogans, and all elements of the visual presentation carefully.*

*You'll be spending thousands of dollars on developing the material and will probably have to live with your choice for several years. If your initial choices grate, you'll have to decide if you can endure them until the materials dwindle, or throw out cartons of untouched materials and replace them with a design you like.*

When you have your "Eureka!" moment and come up with the perfect brand name, supporting logo, mission statement, and brand statement, be sure to protect them legally. Consult with a trademark lawyer to find out which method of registering your brand is appropriate; you can get up to speed at the Library of Congress' copyright center (http://lcweb.loc.gov/copyright) and the U.S. Patent and Trademark Office (www.uspto.gov). Remember, though, that you can only legally protect your unique *expression* of your concept, not the *concept itself*. Someone else may legally come up with his own twist on your concept, but he won't legally be able to mimic your brand or slogan to market it.

## Case Study — ComputerJob Store (part I)

*Please don't think that the ComputerJob Store is a high-tech company. It helps high-tech folks find jobs, and high-tech companies find computer programmers, software developers, and project leaders, and it operates mainly over the Internet (www.computerjobs.com), but that doesn't mean that the company is, at heart, a technology company.*

*"Our strength is building a successful marketing plan and brand awareness," says president Nancy Gilfillan. Her husband, Mike, is chief executive officer. "We're providing candidates to companies looking to fill technology positions, and we don't have a factory in the back producing programmers!"*

*Maybe not, but the Gilfillans hit on a formula for matching up scarce candidates with nerd-hungry employers that's nearly that efficient. Not long after they realized they'd come up with an idea with huge potential, they developed a market strategy that has guided them through several permutations of the service and kept them on course as they've rolled it out nationally.*

*Back in 1992, the Gilfillans were just a couple of programming students at their respective Georgia universities. They met while interning at IBM. Michael decided that after he graduated, he wanted to join a consulting firm that would put him on a series of short-term assignments so that he could get a broad range of experience right away. Nancy followed suit after she graduated, and soon the couple's traditional-career-track former classmates were hounding them to explain how they kept landing plum assignments—and raking in top fees.*

*Michael self-published a guide to Atlanta-area companies that routinely hired contract programmers and peppered it with articles on how to manage a serial-client career, fee ranges for various types of positions and how to work with professional recruiters.*

*The hassles of updating an annual print directory were daunting, so he jumped at the chance to move the project on-line. In February 1995, he wrote a rudimentary web site and placed it with a fledgling web-hosting company called MindSpring (now a nationally known firm), called it Atlanta's ComputerJob Store, and started charging companies to advertise their open positions. By the end of the year, the site had turned a profit and, to their surprise, the Gilfillans had a fast-growing business on their hands.*

*"I didn't fully appreciate the value of our services until we tested an ad in the newspaper and compared that response to what we were doing," says Nancy. The Gilfillans quickly added a resume-posting section to the site and sharpened their requirements for corporate members— they had to provide in-depth technical descriptions of the skills they were seeking, details about the projects, and actual fees instead of a murky "competitive rates" line about their compensation.*

*At the same time, the Gilfillans firmly weeded out the resumes sent their way by nurses, artists, forklift operators and other hopefuls who clearly didn't grasp the tech-only nature of their service. They required qualified individuals to pinpoint their actual availability and specific skill sets so that employers would only get candidates who were qualified and free to take on the project.*

*As they narrowed their scope and deepened the service, the Gilfillans were intuitively creating their unique positioning statement—a matching service that focused exclusively on computer-related positions and those seeking programming related work, in the Atlanta area. Clearly, that fit with the ComputerJob Store brand they'd created for their venture.* (continued on page 84)

# PRODUCT DEVELOPMENT STRATEGIES

Once you've created your company mission statement (or have explicitly recognized the mission you've been pursuing), you can start developing and refining your products or services.

## Importance of New Products

It's far better to change of your own accord and with a purposeful direction, than to be forced into change in reaction to competition and market trends. As a small business owner, you've got an enormous advantage of scale: You're smaller and, therefore, have more intimate relationships with your customers and can respond quickly to their changing needs. By the time larger competitors wake up to a new market reality, you could have saturated the market with your innovation.

It's easier and less risky to do that if you're traveling down a somewhat established path. It's tough for very small companies to pioneer completely new product categories, but it's considerably easier to closely follow a big-company innovator and come up with a clever twist on its mousetrap. Hewlett-Packard and IBM brought personal computers to the business mainstream, but entrepreneur Michael Dell created a billion-dollar company by offering to custom-build PC's for each customer. Now, other PC manufacturers, such as Compaq, and big computer distributors, such as Computer Discount Warehouse, also offer a custom-built option to their customers—but when potential purchasers think of a custom-built PC, they think of Dell.

## Finding a Niche for Your Company

The three classic small business marketing strategies are:

- **Niche expert or dominator** — having deep knowledge of a small slice of the market and seeking to own that slice

- **Follower or improver of competitors' products** — adding your unique twist to an already-established product category

- **Innovative leader** — seeking to introduce completely new products, services or concepts, and growing them quickly to outflank your competition

Usually, small companies adopt a niche or follower strategy. Unless your category is so small or specialized that it can't support more than a handful of companies, it's unlikely that you'll be able to dominate it altogether—at least, not immediately.

As you decide how to position your company, consider the time, money, personnel and energy (compared to your competitors) that you can devote to:

- innovating

- researching and developing new products

- introducing new products

- educating buyers about new products

- marketing campaigns, promotions, and sales efforts

## The Advantages of Being a Niche Expert

Most small business owners instinctively realize that their company is particularly vulnerable to larger competitors with similar products. After all, big companies knock off smaller companies' innovations just as often as the reverse. Minimize David-against-Goliath battles by seeking:

- segments too small or specialized to interest larger competitors

- niche segments that preclude the entry of most larger competitors because of your

  — preemptive technology or expertise

  — local or regional reputation strengths

  — unique distribution methods

- premium-priced or quality or low price or commodity product segments outside the mission of larger companies

# GENERATING NEW PRODUCT IDEAS

As you converse with customers and clients, you'll detect opportunities for new products and variations of existing ones. They're likely to fall into one of these categories:

- **Products that create a new market or niche segment —** Paper disposable diapers are a good example of an entirely new-to-the-world product that, when introduced, created an entirely new and explosively large growth segment for infant care.

- **Additions or line extensions to existing products** — New flavors and new sizes of existing products are examples of line extensions. New LifeSavers flavors continue to proliferate (over 50 to date), continually refreshing a brand name and product line over several decades.

- **Product improvements** — Cars are a good example of products where continuous improvements are made each year, with increased safety, road handling, driver and rider comfort, entertainment feature improvements that competitors strive to quickly copy.

- **Repositioned products** — Tums (the anti-acid stomach product) has successfully repositioned itself to feature its high calcium content as a benefit primarily for women's health needs, along with its original antacid claims.

What do your customers wish they could make your product do? Are they modifying it in some way, or combining it with another product to produce an end result that's new to you? What services do they perform immediately before or after using yours? What are *their* customers asking for—a disposable version? a do-it-yourself kit instead of a by-appointment service? Continually seek ways to reposition, improve, and add on to your core products and services by:

- **periodically screening your products** and comparing them with competitors' products, with an eye towards:

  - improving attributes of products

  - combining the features/benefits of several separate products into a single new product

- **examining users' needs** that are not being met by current competitive products

- **using idea-generating methods like brainstorming**

- **improving a competitor's product**

# Screening Your Current Products

It's tempting to tell yourself, "if it ain't broke, don't fix it." Unfortunately, things can 'break' so gradually that you don't realize they're in bad shape until they're nonfunctional. So that you aren't surprised by a competitor's new product or service that offers attractive new benefits and features to your target market, commit to regularly evaluating your own line. It's smart to continually seek and act on feedback—a topic discussed in more depth in the customer service portion of Chapter 8.

You'll also need to continually measure the performance, price and attributes of your offerings against your direct competitors. Put this on a regular schedule so that even small changes in competitors' offerings won't escape you. Start by establishing a *benchmark* for your own and competitors' products that lists basics such as physical attributes (size, weight, material, color), functions, price, options, distribution methods, guarantees and other relevant data. Then you'll be able to carefully track changes over time.

## Preliminary Product Screening for Small Companies

Here are several tried-and-true methods for evaluating existing products and prototypes:

1. Try out your products with an "expert panel" of internal company personnel (or a panel of knowledgeable business colleagues, if you have no employees) plus external product users. Use a written evaluation form to keep track of results from year to year. An expert panel may also consist of industry experts, consultants, and end users.

2. Add competitors' products to the evaluation with your expert panel of users.

3. Compare evaluations between your company's products and competitors' products, paying particular attention to:

   — differentiation of your products' features and positioning compared to competitive products

   — ability of the competition to develop similar, stronger products

   — cost of pioneering a new product compared to a less-expensive "me-too" introduction

   — your ability to introduce products in the marketplace compared to a competitor's ability to defend markets

4. Decide if your company needs to make improvements. Key question: How will your competitor's improvements in products affect your sales?

5. Screen existing products against pre-established company criteria:

— your company's mission, ethics and philosophy, and strategies

— your company's operational expertise and distribution methods

— future company business goals and product categories

— company customer and buyer profiles

— company sales volume, share, and profitability objectives

— company ability to invest in new technology or marketing spending

6. Outline an action plan with an affordable budget. Obviously, you won't want to take any action that will not positively affect sales of your products and boost your market share.

7. Decide if qualitative and quantitative market research is necessary, depending upon the technology and expense to retool and introduce an improved product. The greater the risk, the more valuable qualitative and quantitative market research may prove.

8. Conduct a trial market test with product users or key trade contacts for evaluation.

9. Retool, retest, rethink, reposition, as necessary.

## Case Study — ComputerJob Store (part II)

*Of course, the Gilfillans couldn't hide the ComputerJob Store from the rest of the world—after all, it was right out there on the Internet for everyone to see. In 1996, they opened a section of the site for Dallas, and added Chicago and the Carolinas in 1997. Venture capital financing accelerated their expansion to Florida, Washington, DC, and New York City. A national section embraces all regions not otherwise served.*

*While theirs was one of the very first career sites on the Internet, they've chosen to dominate their niche, not become a general career site with hundreds of thousands of jobs and resumes. At press time, the site listed 25,000 active resumes and 20,000 open positions. By focusing only on computer jobs, the Gilfillans are both mining one of the most profitable segments of the job-matching category and developing content, such as salary surveys, that is very meaningful to their target audiences—and keeps users coming back.*

*Opening the service to each new metropolitan area isn't as easy as just slapping up a new section to the web site. The Gilfillans actively recruit corporate subscribers even as they're waiting for a critical mass of resumes in that area to filter in. Once they have 1,000 resumes, they officially open a section for that metropolitan area. They immediately blitz the region with billboard, direct mail, newspaper and trade journal ads to stir up interest in the service and encourage even more programmers to post their resumes and corporations to subscribe. Sure, they advertise on big Internet search sites, but it's their aim to raise awareness virtually overnight as they enter each region—and that takes all kinds of media.*

*"Once we drive people to the site, they'll quickly see that we're serving their area," says Nancy. "We have a formula for entering a new region—we know about how much money it will cost to market there until it pays for itself."*

*Meanwhile, the ComputerJob Store story is filtering out in national trade, computer and business journals through the efforts of the public relations agency that is consistently sending out press releases and pitching stories to reporters and editors who cover the computer and career beats. When a major computer magazine profiled the service, the Gilfillans noticed an immediate increase in traffic on the site.*

*The Gilfillans have also concocted a formula for extracting as much revenue as each market will bear. In Atlanta, still their largest market, they charge as much as $2,000 for a corporation that's constantly reviewing incoming resumes for its positions. Small companies in still-developing markets might pay as little as $50 a week to place an ad on the site.*

*This strategy has set them on an upward growth spiral that is reinforced, not diluted, as they expand nationally. The Gilfillans are adding services that will allow corporate clients to buy one access to one resume at a time—a premium service that they can charge top dollar for; one that also addresses the desire of weary corporate recruiters to zero in on just the perfect candidate. They're also considering ways to add computer-related, non-programming jobs. And after that? Given that their model allows them to turn a profit from a new market soon after entering it, they're not afraid to say that they intend to take the ComputerJob Store global.*

# Examining Users' Needs

Small companies are often discouraged about product development because of the perceived difficulty, time, and expense ("...only really *big* companies can afford to do it!"). It's not as daunting as it seems. Use all the eyes, ears and brains of your company to gather feedback from:

- **Customers** — Ask them what they want or need that they're not getting from anyone else. What new problems are starting to emerge that you might solve for them?

- **End users** — Make sure you often talk with the end users of your product, especially if they are not the same people who actually buy your product. Often, sales assistants can meet with end-users casually in the office or over coffee when they accompany salespeople to customer or client sites. Or, have sales staffers regularly interview end users over the phone.

- **Your sales force** — Collect observations from your sales force about, or do your own investigating into, new market innovations or emerging opportunities. Challenge sales staffers to come up with leading questions to ask their customers and to look for the impact of specific market trends on your customers.

- **Your suppliers** — They're often the closest to the latest technology, materials, ingredients, international advances, and competitive improvements. Don't hesitate to ask them to give you a no-holds-barred evaluation of your product or service—after all, if their feedback results in an innovation that improves sales, you've both gained.

# Inventing New Ideas

You've probably got more ideas than you know what to do with already. The difference between a great idea and a great product or service is often just a matter of timing and execution. Keep files of your flashes of inspiration. Then, regularly feed them with market data that adds credibility to them and explores ways to bring them to market.

Generate and hone your ideas by:

- keeping up with the views of industry and technology experts by attending seminars, reading books and magazine articles, and participating in online chats and newsgroups

- finding and interviewing new product pioneer users in categories related to yours

- conducting a feature and benefit analysis of your company's products and competitive products, then adding new features that are important to users while dropping less popular ones

- conducting group "brainstorming" sessions

## Work Smart

*Brainstorming only works if everyone in the small group (no more than 10):*

- *agrees on the specific topic*

- *respects every idea tossed out, no matter how impractical or silly it may initially appear (and respects each participant)*

- *is willing to mix and match bits and pieces of different ideas without regard to personal "ownership"*

- *takes group credit for the more polished, edited idea that eventually emerges.*

*You'll likely need a moderator to enforce the ground rules, and a secretary to write down the ideas and lead the editing process. Brainstorming sessions can be intense, so it's best to keep each one to an hour. Schedule sessions over several days if you're tackling a big concept.*

## Improving a Competitor's Product

Sometimes the best, least expensive, fastest, and least risky way to introduce new products is to copy or improve upon a competitor's new product introduction.

Many companies, large and small, consciously adapt a strategy to "follow the leader" when it comes to new product introduction, pricing and other business changes. This can save expensive R&D costs and redirect those funds toward educating the target buyers.

To successfully follow in another company's footsteps, you'll need to:

- be able to move quickly to commit company resources to capitalize on a competitor's new products

- compete in product categories where innovation does not necessarily depend upon proprietary technology, large capital improvements, and preemptive patents to protect new ideas

- often settle for less sales potential than the innovator

- be careful to not simply become reactive and lose sight of your own marketing goals and company

- make sure there are no infringements on patent or copyrights in the product, its packaging, branding, and mode of delivery

### It Worked for Them!

*A California company began offering hard-to-find baby gear, safety gadgets (such as cabinet latches) and unusual educational toys through a mail-order catalog. One mother who received the catalog was a brand manager for a large packaged food company. After researching the market in her spare time, she decided that*  *the size of the market could support two catalogs offering similar and, in many cases, the very same products.*

*Her knockoff catalog targeted a slightly less affluent customer and had a less expensive look than the original, and suppliers generally considered the effort to be a perennial second-place contender. She didn't care; she built a profitable company with millions in annual sales by closely following in the wake of the category leader.*

# NEW PRODUCT CONCEPT SCREENING

A small company often survives on its reputation with key customers, which can be threatened or weakened with product development failures. Minimize the chance of having a product backfire on you by evaluating it against several key criteria.

## Using Your Company's Marketing Strategies

Concept screening against new or pre-existing company marketing strategies will reinforce your focus and make sure you don't waste your resources on a dud. Use scarce resources to successfully introduce new products. First, make sure the new product or service is consistent with your target buyer, company mission, and brand image. How does the product or service introduction:

- help translate the company mission into a measurable annual objective

- enhance the image and credibility of products you already produce

- anticipate or respond to market trends and competitors' innovations

## Projecting Sales and Profitability Minimums

If you haven't already, figure the minimum gross margin that the new product or service must bring in to meet your corporate profitability and growth goals. (The gross margin is the sale price minus the actual cost of producing the product or service. Gross margin covers administrative, marketing, other overhead, taxes, and net profit.)

## Listening to Key Customers and Buyers

Current customers and clients have a vested interest in your success, so it's smart to solicit their comments and ideas as you refine your new concept's design, features, and price.

# NEW PRODUCT PROTOTYPES

Call it what you will—prototype, mock-up or trial run—but you'll definitely want to create a full-sized trial model of your product or service so that you and a selected panel of customers, clients, and end users can take it through its paces before you unveil it to the wide world.

---

### Preliminary Checklist for Product Prototype Development

*Check with key consumers or buyers to be sure that the features and benefits of your prototype deliver as promised, and meet the end users' needs. Be sure that:*

❑ *Packaging, pricing and brand positioning fulfill the concept targets.*

❑ *Manufacturing, sales and distribution are achievable and manageable with your company's resources.*

❑ *You have at least the minimum resources needed to successfully introduce the new product into the competitive environment and targeted market segment.*

❑ *New product features and benefits can be accurately communicated to the target buyer group.*

❑ *Your company can enjoy new product exclusivity long enough to recoup development investment and achieve company growth, sales and profit objectives for the new product.*

---

# TESTING PACKAGING AND PRICING

No one wants to bring to market a product with the wrong type of packaging, the wrong price and confusing marketing support.

## Package Testing

New products and their packaging should be tested under real-life conditions for:

- storage under varying temperatures, lighting and humidity

- shipping through all distribution channels, with roughest handling

- retail environment tests under sun and fluorescent lighting conditions

- shelf life studies for age deterioration

## Price Testing

New product pricing should be examined for:

- competitive advantage (how is your product a better value than the competitor's?)

---

- parity in relation to competitors (are you getting as much for your product as your competitor, considering differences in features and benefits?)

- premiums compared to competitors with similar products or substitutes (in other words, are your customers paying more for the extra value they receive?)

- adequate margins for:

  — distributor and wholesaler pricing

  — marketing spending support

  — post-sale customer support

  — profits

- consistency with brand positioning (meaning products positioned as *upscale* are more expensive than similar products positioned as *mass market*.)

# MEASURING SUCCESS OF NEW PRODUCTS

Once you've introduced a new product or service, or developed significant improvements to existing ones, you'll naturally want to do some follow-up to measure the success of the project. Whether the introduction is ultimately successful or not, you need to be able to learn from the process to achieve more success down the line. Big companies track the progress of new products and services by conducting extensive consumer and user studies, creating simulated market tests, and extensively measuring customer reaction in controlled test markets. If full-fledged tests are outside your scope, adapt these concepts by:

- Talking to buyers and consumers about product satisfaction and purchases. From a marketing research standpoint, this is biased, qualitative research without standard interview controls. But it is timely information and you may be able to act on it immediately.

- Conduct a test of advertising spending levels in different test markets or, with a single business in one location, over different time periods. It is relatively easy to vary introductory spending in each market, if you are testing a number of geographical markets. Make sure that the differences in advertising spending are significant—at least 50 percent more or less than the benchmark for each type of media.

- Examine weekly company sales receipts for new account sales, compared to receipts for reorders. This is an indirect, but free, way to measure initial purchase compared to reorder sales.

# Chapter 6

# Packaging and Pricing Your Product

As appealing as your products and services are, people will still want to know how much they'll have to pay to acquire them. Price your offerings too high, and you'll alienate much of your potential market. Price too low, and you'll soon be running in the red and won't be able to offer any products or services at all.

Packaging is closely related to pricing. The size and form in which customers receive your offering is closely entwined with customers' perceptions of value. Fancifully packaged gourmet food items often sell for a premium, while house-brand breakfast cereal contained in a plain cardboard box is perceived for the generic value it is. Services are packaged, too, as it were; providers need to decide what increments they'll charge for—by the hour, the project, retainer, or a percentage of the money that the client saved by taking a consultant's advice. The permutations are nearly as varied as the number of service businesses.

It's tempting to simply call a bunch of competitors or go to a trade association, find out what the market rate is, and plump yourself in the middle. However, pricing and packaging are intrinsically marketing functions. Your product's price and package are shorthand signals to prospective clients about how you are positioning yourself in the market. If they become familiar with what you're selling and then hear a high price, they'll want to know what they'll get for the extra amount they pay and especially how that compares to similar products or services that are priced less. If your price strikes people as a terrific bargain, they may wonder if you're cutting corners; will they be disappointed to "get what they pay for?"

Once you do set a price, customers will quickly become accustomed to it; the price was one factor they considered and accepted when they *became* customers. You'll undermine their loyalty if you constantly experiment with different pricing schemes. Starting low and then raising prices, without a dramatic increase in the quality or amount of what you're selling for that price, will surprise and alienate people. Starting high and then dropping prices could offend people who bought at the higher price—and then wonder if they were suckers. Better to research pricing and packaging and set the right price from the beginning.

# PACKAGE DESIGN

Of course, the specifics of your offering dictate the essentials of the package. Consumer goods always need to be in a self-explanatory package that reiterates what the product is, what it will do for the purchaser, ingredients and other marketing copy. High-tech products may come in a shrink-wrapped cardboard box, but actually be bundled with a human installation expert who figures heavily into the total package even if he isn't shrink-wrapped along with the physical product.

Services are packaged not only in the form of the price structure, but also with the way that the service is delivered. Garage mechanics typically wear uniforms signaling their affiliation with the garage; an upscale bed-and-breakfast might offer guests hospitality baskets featuring sample sizes of locally made soap, candy and candles. Consulting companies strive to differentiate themselves with their packages of services by bundling areas of expertise together, such as tax return preparation and estate-planning sessions for a single introductory fee. A motivational speaker may not wear his logo on his suit, but it is likely to be plastered over all the registration material, signs, handouts, folders, and follow-up tapes and books he sells in conjunction with his appearances. Any way that the company logo, slogan and image can be conveyed through people, mode of distribution or related products reinforces the packaging, as it were, of services.

In any event, package design essentials apply to both service and physical-product companies, and must fulfill these goals:

- reflect the business positioning

- communicate graphic identity

- reflect target buyer values

## Package Designs for Positioning

The unique collection of brand or business values that differentiates your business from the competition is known as positioning. Packaging designs should communicate the business' positioning or unique set of values. An upscale boutique probably will find fancy gift boxes and oversized full-color shopping bags an essential element of the shopper's experience, while those same customers are more than happy to use recycled plastic grocery bags as they pack their own ripe tomatoes at their subdivision's weekly farmer's market. The demographics and lifestyle of the customer haven't changed, but the expectation of the packaging provided by the seller shifts to reflect the product, price and sophistication of the seller.

Unless you're already experienced at choosing packaging, hire an industrial designer, package designer or graphic designer to help you. Don't overlook safety issues such as childproof caps on herbal supplements and self-closing lids on tubs of industrial solvents. Be sure you find out what regulatory and safety guidelines you need to comply with; for instance, it's now common (and smart) to urge users to **not** recycle plastic tubs that have held chemicals for other industrial or household use.

The fun part is working with your designer to develop the look of the package. Choose colors that coordinate with your corporate image but also convey a sense of the product—icy silver to imply the space-age features of a high-tech product, perhaps, or maybe cartoon-like characters to convey how easy that product is to use.

## Case Study — Outdated Packaging and Distribution

*A leading manufacturer and distributor of African-American hair care and beauty products realized that its outdated packaging and distribution methods were actually discouraging retailers and beauty salons from ordering. While several splashy new products were being developed and tested, the company's president decided to clean house to give the new lines the strongest possible start.*

*Because sparring brand managers each demanded their own lines of custom-designed bottles, boxes and sizes for their product lines, the company had hundreds of variations on its basic brands—and few economies of scale in ordering bottles and packaging. That fragmentation backed into the production line, because workers were constantly interrupting the product manufacturing and filling lines to change containers. Simply by streamlining the number and styles of containers for the various brands, and then making corresponding changes in the labeling and organization of the warehouse, the company president cut the time it takes to fill a customer's order from 10 days to four.*

*The next step was to persuade customers that it would benefit them to install bar coding hardware and software that would feed information back to the manufacturer. Many small salons didn't want to spend the money, but the manufacturer was able to demonstrate to them how they'd be able to better control their cash by ordering smaller amounts, more frequently, because the flow of electronic data back to the warehouse would automatically trigger a reorder query. When they realized that the manufacturer would be shouldering some of the inventory headache, most of the salons and stores signed on.*

## Designing for Graphic Identity

Your designer will probably start talking right away about creating a corporate graphic identity. In other words, it's important that all materials you produce, from business cards to box inserts, literally look as though they belong together. You may want to integrate your logo on package labels and boxes, and let each line or brand have its own look. Or if you're selling services or information, you may simply want to create subtle variations on the logo as your graphic identity. Well-known consumer brands splash their graphic identities over ads, commercials and packaging so thoroughly that we know at a glance if a can of pop is a Coke or a Pepsi, for instance.

A strong graphic identity can put you on the map in a retail outlet. You have to pay for some sort of packaging, labels and tags anyway—work closely with your designer to pack as much punch as you can.

## Packaging to Reflect Buyer's Values

The look and the copy on the package need to speak the same language as the potential buyer. The more you know about your potential buyer, the better you'll be able to design a package that reflects his or her values and buying motivations—and make it likely that the packaging will become a key element of your selling equation.

### Case Study — Garden.com

 *Cliff Sharples kept graphic design in mind as he developed Garden.com, one of the most successful Internet retail sites. The online garden supply store was started in 1997 by Sharples and a small group of entrepreneurs specifically to gain the loyalty and dollars of the millions of American amateur gardeners.*

*Because gardeners crave a wide variety of plants and accessories, and because they avidly seek out and consume information that will help them produce flowers, vegetables, landscaping or just a decent lawn, Sharples knew that the products he'd offer had to be surrounded by detailed, authoritative content. He hired a nationally known garden magazine editor and gave him free rein to develop articles ranging from the history of plants to garden design to tips on how to prevent root rot.*

*Garden.com is redefining the way green thumbs buy plants, tools, accessories, books and gifts. The site blends state-of-the-art electronic direct marketing techniques with lush pictures of flowers and other products, and extensive editorial content that's exhaustively cross-referenced with those products. If a surfer is interested in planting flowering shrubs, he can read articles about gardens that feature them; review descriptions of various types of shrubs and the conditions they need to flourish; buy fertilizer, a shovel and a book about caring for those shrubs; pay by credit card—and have it all delivered to his front porch.*

*As you'd expect, Garden.com's basic color is green. Fun-with-dirt logos, such as a wheelbarrow "shopping cart," reinforce the theme.*

*Traditional gardening stores, of course, have the advantage not only of immediate gratification, but also the sensual atmosphere of live plants, flowers and earth. Traditional direct-mail plant nurseries usually differentiate themselves by providing very in-depth information about the stock they sell. To distinguish Garden.com from these two well-entrenched categories of competition, Sharples and his team are cultivating a very distinctive graphic style that pervades the web site and is carried through to the unusual lime-green corrugated gift boxes and multi-reuse wood-shaving packing material.*

*Customer service—a weak point for many online retailers—isn't just left up to the tender mercies of e-mail and the webmaster. Customers' inquiries and problems are handled by phone or e-mail, depending on their complexity and urgency, so that consumers have the reassurance of talking to a "real" person. As it expands, Garden.com will continue to package its products and services in unique ways.*

# PRICING YOUR PRODUCT

The ideal price for any product or service is one that is acceptable to both buyer and seller.

From the buyer's standpoint, the right price is a function of product purchase value and other competitive choices in the marketplace. Quite literally, buyers ask themselves, "Is this product or service worth the price?"

Things are more complicated from the seller's point of view. The universal business goal is to price products to maximize both sales and profits, while providing enough margin to take care of applicable marketing and overhead expenses.

Assuming that you've already analyzed the size and characteristics of your potential market, you'll likely follow these steps to arrive at the right price:

1. Analyze the size and composition of your target market

2. Research price elasticity for your product

3. Evaluate your product's uniqueness

4. Select your channels of distribution (explained in Chapter 7)

5. Consider product life cycles

6. Analyze your costs and overhead

7. Estimate sales at different prices

8. Consider secondary pricing strategies

9. Select final pricing levels

# Analyzing Size and Composition of Market

How much you sell—the volume of sales—is a major factor in determining the price of each item or element of service. If you're manufacturing goods, the more you can sell, the less you might charge for each one; gross profits will grow with overall volume.

Because services depend on actual people to perform them (automation notwithstanding), you can only offer more services by also expanding the number of people who can deliver those services. To be sure, you will gain substantial advantages by increasing sales volume and spreading the cost of overhead (including marketing) over that volume, but unless you've figured out a way to clone workers, your cost structure will be anchored by the amount you must pay your workers to deliver those services.

Of course, find out as much as you can about what your competitors charge, what their sales volume is, and any other insights that will help you understand how much money they are actually making, and how. Pay special attention to premium- and bargain-priced competitors and their market shares. You may find a price point that's overlooked which you can successfully claim. Be sure, though, that the niche is overlooked and not abandoned by former competitors who priced themselves out of the market in either direction.

# Researching Product Price Elasticity

If demand for your product or service changes significantly with slight changes in price, the product category is considered to be **elastic** with respect to price. If no significant volume changes occur, even with significant price changes, the category is **inelastic**.

## Work Smart

*Grocery staples, such as flour and paper towels, are usually very price sensitive. Charge ten percent more than the competition on the same shelf and your products will languish; charge 10 percent less and you may not be able to keep up with demand, alienating the store buyers. This is an elastic category.*

*On the other hand, gourmet food specialties are often inelastic. Stores even within the same market may charge as much as 50 percent more or less for the identical chutney or Cajun relish, but if a shopper wants that chutney or relish, he's likely to buy it regardless of the price he's facing at the moment. Consumers shopping these premium-priced categories are not as value-conscious as shoppers in a regular grocery store environment—though those very same shoppers may be the ones that clean you out of your bargain paper towels.*

What does price elasticity mean for product pricing? The greater the price elasticity, the closer you should price your products to similar competitive products and vice versa. While your product may be unique, consumers will not pay much of a premium for it if there are similar competitive choices at lower prices. Rely on research about your market category and trade group data to keep you clued in about changes in elasticity in your market.

# Evaluating Your Product's Uniqueness

The closer your product resembles competitive products, the smaller the price differences that buyers will tolerate. And the closer the product differences between brands, the greater the probability that the category is price-elastic, and that brand switching will occur when products go on sale.

---

**Work Smart**

*You may be utterly persuaded of the uniqueness of your product or service—but consumers have to catch on, too, or they won't pay more for it. Depending upon the category, very unique products may or may not be readily accepted by buyers.*

*Our chutney buyers from the previous example are more concerned with putting together the perfect weekend meal to impress their in-laws than they are with price; the chutney reflects their personal style and values in a way that super-sopping paper towels do not.*

---

Retail shelves are so crowded that it's hard for a new product to stand out from the established brands. Catching consumers' attention long enough to persuade them of the unique differences of your product is a real challenge. Similarly, many services are in crowded categories where it's hard to stand out. Janitorial services are so generic that only an unusual approach (for instance, if you had employees with allergies and needed a service that used only organic cleaning compounds) will stand out. People are likely to shop for and buy on price.

If you're not sure how to price your product or service, you will probably want to field-test several different prices on a limited basis. By experimenting with different combinations of prices and marketing messages, you'll no doubt hit on the one that most efficiently persuades consumers of the price-value of your offering.

## Case Study — Universal Advisory Services

*Universal Advisory Services, a New Mexico financial services firm, doesn't introduce new services without doing its homework. President Joseph Kopczynski keeps close track of the company's key demographic groups—mainly small business owners and retirees—and periodically calls randomly selected groups of customers to ask, "We're considering offering this kind of service. Do you have any interest in it, and how do you think it would go over with your peer group?"*

*While Universal's services are often delivered face-to-face with clients, Kopczynski relies heavily on referrals from his network of attorneys and certified public accountants. He hosts regular lunches in the office, or golf outings, to run new ideas by some of his network peers. However, he always makes sure that they understand he's asking only for advice, and won't be actually pitching them any new services during the get-together.*

*Their advice has proved invaluable. "We struggled for three years with wondering how to price our services," he says. "We do so many things (for customers) and we believe that we add a lot of value, but we felt that we weren't being paid adequately for what we brought to the table."*

*Instead of charging by the hour, as most financial advisory firms do, Kopczynski pondered switching to a percentage-of-net-worth formula. That would encourage Universal's planners to take a big-picture view for clients with large, complicated portfolios that included businesses, real estate, collectibles and investments. Those with less complex needs would still be charged by the hour. With the help of his informal advisors, Kopczynski fine-tuned his explanation of the fee structure change. He also reassigned staff advisors so that they were matched with the fee structure that best fit their own consulting styles.*

*The result: Key clients agreed to try out the new structure, and after a few months, most realized that the more holistic advice they were getting had a measurably positive impact on the performance of their portfolios.*

# Considering Product Life Cycles

The shorter the time that your product or service is available to the market, the greater the impact on price. Items available seasonally and rarely are likely to garner a higher price than those readily available any time, through many stores and distribution channels

Personal computer software, for instance, is often outmoded within six months of its official release. Product pricing cycles have accelerated to match, with introductory pricing decreasing to significantly lower levels only six to eight months later.

These continuously evolving high-tech categories make it difficult for companies to recover development costs, accurately predict sales volume, afford planned marketing support, and price products accurately in relation to a competitor's products.

# Analyzing Your Costs and Overhead

The most common errors in pricing are:

- pricing products or services based only on the cost to produce them

- pricing products based only on competitors' prices

A thoroughly thought-out pricing structure takes into account these factors:

1. Covering the cost of producing the goods or services

2. Covering marketing and overhead expenses

3. Enabling profit objectives

4. Ability to afford distribution margin discounts.

5. Ability to afford the sales commissions.

6. Strategically placing the product in its market.

## Breakeven Analysis

A breakeven analysis is a commonly used method that focuses on the volume of sales at which total revenues will equal total costs. The idea is to set the price of a unit of product or service at a level where it will cover all of its own variable costs (material, labor, marketing etc.) plus its portion of the fixed costs of the company (overhead).

At the point where enough units have been sold to cover all fixed and variable costs, breakeven is achieved. After that point, the sales price of a unit sold minus the variable (direct) cost to produce it equals pure profit, which can be taken as income to the company's owners or reinvested in equipment, marketing or other capital-hungry expansion efforts.

For example, a case of bottled tea beverages in 12-ounce ready-to-drink bottles has a cost of goods of $3.82 per case of 12. Factory price to distributors is $6.54/case. Gross margin (price minus cost of goods) is $2.72/case. If the company's fixed costs (e.g., overhead, factory expenses, etc.) are estimated at $75,000.00 per year, then the breakeven point would be 27,573.5 cases of tea ($75,000 divided by $2.72/case).

| Breakeven Analysis Model | |
|---|---|
| Variable (direct) cost | $3.82 per case |
| Factory price | $6.54 per case |
| Gross margin (price - cost of goods) | $2.72 per case<br>($6.54 - $3.82) |
| Fixed costs | $75,000.00 per year |
| Breakeven point<br>(fixed costs ÷ gross margin) | 27,573.5 cases<br>($75,000.00 ÷ $2.72 per case) |

## Consumer Goods Pricing

Consumer goods experts suggest the estimated cost of goods should be no more than 15 percent of the suggested retail price because margins of 55 percent to 65 percent are usually needed to cover gross profit.

In turn, the gross profit must cover:

- overhead

- marketing spending support (typically 10 to 20 percent of sales)

- broker commissions (typically 5 to 10 percent of net sales)

- your own company profits

The remainder of the retail sales price is usually split evenly between the wholesalers or distributors who sell to retail stores and the retailers themselves, to allow them a sufficient markup to cover *their* gross margins.

| Consumer Goods Pricing Model | |
|---|---|
| Retail price of 32-ounce shampoo | $2.99 per bottle |
| Cost of goods per unit (15% of selling of retail price) | $0.4485 per bottle |
| Company unit price with 64.5% gross margin ($0.4485 = 35.5% of unit price) | $1.256 per bottle<br>($0.4485 ÷ 35.5%) |
| Distributor unit price to retailers with 30% distributor margin ($1.256 = 70% of distributor price) | $1.794 per bottle<br>($1.256 ÷ 70%) |
| Retail unit price with 40% retail margin ($1.794 = 60% of retail price) | $2.99 per bottle<br>($1.794 ÷ 60%) |

## Service Sector and Other Industry Pricing

Many other industries, such as restaurants, other retail establishments and consulting services, historically operate on the "keystone" pricing principle:

- The cost of goods is limited to 33 percent, or one-third of retail prices.

- Labor and overhead is limited to another 33 percent of retail prices.

- Gross profits are a minimum of 33 percent of retail prices. (Emphasis on gross! Remember that taxes, interest and overhead expenses must be deducted before net profits are determined.)

However, as services proliferate, some companies are making their pricing structure a very distinct element of their marketing and market positioning. For instance, some management consulting firms that help companies reorganize or re-engineer will first create a benchmark profit analysis, then complete the project. After an agreed-upon time has passed, they'll redo the profit analysis, determine the exact time and money saved (and gained) because of their prescient advice, and collect a portion of that as their fee.

## Wholesaling and Retailing Markups

If you're in retailing or wholesaling, be sure you understand the not-so-semantic difference between "markups" and "markdowns" in your category's commonly understood pricing structure. Retailers and wholesalers need to consider the issue of markups in their pricing structure, and manufacturers or other product producers need to be aware of the average markup in their industry.

A markup is the percentage of the selling price (or sometimes the cost) of a product which is added to the cost in order to arrive at a selling price. Be aware that there are two different ways to calculate markup—on cost or on selling price. So when you ask someone, "What's your markup on that item?" it won't help to get an answer of "20 percent." You need to know 20 percent of cost or 20 percent of selling price.

In retailing, the industry standard is to compute markup as a percentage of selling price. Let's say a store owner purchases a crate of clocks for which he pays $12 each. He intends to add $4 and sell them for $16 each. The markup percentage on cost is the dollar markup ($4.00) divided by the cost ($12.00), for a 33 percent markup.

However, if the markup is calculated on the selling price, it's the dollar markup ($4.00) divided by the selling price ($16.00), for a 25 percent markup.

"Markdowns" are considerably easier to figure; they're simply a percentage less than the highest actual selling price.

As a product wends its way through a distribution channel, each step along the journey adds a markup before selling the product to the next step.

Here's an example of how markups work based on selling price, in which the producer of the item sells it to the wholesaler for $25; the wholesaler to the retailer for $35; and retailer to the consumer for $50.

| Selling Price Markup Model | | | |
|---|---|---|---|
| Distribution outlet | Pricing formula | Cost in dollars | Percentage of cost |
| Producer | Cost | 20.00 | 80.0 |
| | Markup | 5.00 | 20.0 |
| | Selling Price | 25.00 | 100.0 |
| Wholesale Outlet | Cost | 25.00 | 71.5 |
| | Markup | 10.00 | 28.5 |
| | Selling Price | 35.00 | 100.0 |
| Retailer | Cost | 35.00 | 70.0 |
| | Markup | 15.00 | 30.0 |
| | Selling Price | 50.00 | 100.0 |

Markups vary widely among industries. For example, average markups (on selling price in these cases) are around 14 percent on tobacco products, 50 percent on greeting cards, 8 percent on baby food and often more than 50 percent on high-end meats.

Markups, like all pricing strategies, depend on three influences—cost, competition and demand.

# Estimating Sales at Different Prices

Once you've scoped out the tolerance of your target market for various price points and the elasticity of prices in your category, factor in your company's operational costs and growth objectives. Consider:

- cost of goods

- marketing spending

- overhead

- sales commissions

- distributor markups

- shipping costs to distributors

- profit objectives

Pricing at different levels to generate different volume levels may not address benchmark company objectives. Pricing must cover all costs, spending and margin objectives.

# Considering Other Pricing Strategies

You can use pricing as a weapon or a defense, too. You may want to undercut a consumer's loyalty to a certain competing product by offering periodic discounts on your product that are so attractive that consumers can't help but try yours. Or you may have a policy of *never* discounting because you believe it would cheapen the brand image.

A good pricing strategy indicates guidelines for action in the case of price increases or decreases. For example, "We will price at or near the share leader's pricing on a per unit basis. We will increase prices to follow a share leader price increase, but only to preserve margin objectives."

Strategically, you may want to consider temporarily delaying necessary price increases driven by supplier and ingredient price increases. Take affordable, smaller profit margins if your category segment is price elastic. If competitors are increasing prices and your company decides not to, this could be a temporary advantage for your company since sales volume may increase.

## Case Study — Maas Polishing Cream

*A little can of polishing cream made an instant entrepreneur out of Donna Maas.*

*She was vacationing in Germany in 1992 when she picked up a can of polishing cream that was safe for any surface—including those, like fiberglass, that shouldn't come within shouting distance of abrasives. Impressed, Maas acquired the rights to produce and distribute the cream in North America. Figuring out how to package it was easy: Tubes were the most user-friendly, easy to pack and ship, and the cheapest alternative.*

*It was tougher for Maas (who named the cream after herself) to focus on her initial markets. She tested advertising in motorcycle magazines and with airline manufacturers and got an enthusiastic response. A one-hour appearance on the Home Shopping Club resulted in instantaneous sales of 17,000 tubes. In her third year of business, sales skyrocketed 800 percent.*

*Even as Maas Polishing Cream was pummeling its competitors and new market niches (gun owners, boat owners) emerged with tiresome regularity, Maas was worried that the runaway growth would eclipse her relationship with distributors, who had exclusive regional rights, and large retailers. Instead of setting a single per-case price, she decided to capitalize on the fact that different distribution channels and submarkets had different tolerances for price. Jewelers, who sold Maas Polishing Cream in small tubes, wanted to maintain an aura of exclusivity around it. On the other hand, mass merchants, who were selling large-sized containers, were more concerned about the best possible price.*

*Maas researched and developed specific profiles for each of her submarkets and then set prices that reflected not just the ability of some consumers to pay more, but the images that her widely varying distributors wanted to maintain. "They get personalized information from me that explains how this price best fits their market. That has helped me develop relationships with them," says Maas.*

## Selecting Final Pricing Levels

Final pricing levels for products should have flexibility for both increases and discounts to customers. Price increases may be inevitable because of component, ingredient and processing cost increases. Service firms may have to increase wages to its rank and file, forcing a rise in fees.

As with physics, for every pricing action, there's an equal and opposite reaction. If you have to raise your price, even for reasons outside your control, be prepared for customers to balk and for sales to drop off. They may decide to drink tea if coffee prices spike, or to fill out their own tax forms if the local accounting firm doubles its hourly rate.

Similarly, brace yourself for sudden price fluctuations if your competitors are warring with you and each other for market share. Consumers will have a field day, but your profit margins may be buffeted by the price wars.

Chapter **7**

# Choosing Distribution Methods

Distribution is more than just "getting it out the door." Not only is your distribution method intrinsically linked with your product packaging and pricing strategy, but it also communicates to your customers your company's philosophy of customer relationship.

It used to be that distribution was a linear progression for any company. Manufacturers received raw materials, produced finished goods and shipped them out with a one-way ticket. Service companies sized up a client's situation, made a proposal on how they'd complete the service, did it and bowed out.

With outsourcing now a permanent part of many companies' operations, suppliers no longer are expected to just do the simple job and stay out of the way. Manufacturers are often expected to micromanage their production lines, shipping departments and distribution methods with a constant flow of electronic data between them and their customers.

When a customer is running low on the item you supply, you'd better have more ready, or you're holding up the entire supply chain. Similarly, service companies are expected to constantly scan the horizon for more efficient, less expensive ways to deliver their services, and to anticipate when clients might need them. Even a low-tech maid service can use distribution as a marketing tool by asking customers if they'd like to squeeze in extra scourings between holiday parties, and then adjusting their workers' schedules accordingly.

Manufacturers face a dizzying array of distribution channels, including:

- **retail outlets** owned by your company or by an independent merchant or chain

- **wholesale outlets** of your own or those of independent distributors or brokers

- **individual sales people,** compensated by salary, commission, or both

- **direct mail** via your own catalog or flyers

- **telemarketing** on your own or through a contract firm

- **selling direct** through your own Internet site or through a mall or online affiliate

- **auctioning** new goods or seconds via your own Internet site or a general auction site

- **TV and cable** direct marketing and home shopping channels

Thanks to the Internet, services are finding greater flexibility in distribution, including:

- **one-on-one sessions** conducted at your site (such as a dry cleaner) or at the client's site (such as individualized software training)

- **small group** sessions and discussions

- **large group** lectures, conventions

- **subscription** videoconferencing or teleconferencing

- **online** sites, forums and exchanges

- **combining several** of these methods with books, tapes, do-it-yourself kits and other methods that enable the client to continue with the material at his own pace and in his own space

While there are many tried-and-true channels of distribution, innovations emerge every day in nearly every arena. Even if your competitors have conditioned your target market to receive a product or service in a particular format, don't be afraid to test alternatives. You may come up with a whole new business model—just as Amazon.com, ebay.com and other Internet retailers are doing.

First, analyze the modes of distribution currently favored by your target market. Start by:

1. **Identifying how competitors' products are sold** — For decades, Avon Products clung to its once-powerful army of Avon ladies to sell its mid-priced cosmetics and fragrances.

Now, Avon is surprising its old customers, and gaining new ones, by jumping into another tried-and-true channel—kiosks in department stores and malls.

2. **Analyze strengths, weaknesses, opportunities and threats for your business** — The new retail store strategy is pitting Avon head-to-head with entrenched department store cosmetic standard-bearers such as Clinique and Estee Lauder. Avon executives are convinced that they'll win market share based on price, value and the company's reputation.

3. **Examine costs of channels and sales force options** — Avon is spending upwards of $70,000 for each custom-built wood-and-chrome kiosk and now has to hire platoons of salaried sales employees—something it has never done before.

4. **Determine which distribution options match your overall marketing strategy** — Avon is determined to claim a portion of the higher-end cosmetics category for its own. Its old-time Avon ladies very rarely called on department-store clientele.

5. **Prioritize your distribution choices** — Avon is making a splash with the kiosks in very high-profile malls located, not coincidentally, in towns where magazine editors and writers tend to live. Meanwhile, it's also revamping materials for its tens of thousands of Avon ladies.

# HOW ARE COMPETITORS' PRODUCTS SOLD?

It can be confusing to sort out exactly who your direct competitors are. After all, your target market might be able to get products or services similar to yours in a variety of ways. A small residential architectural firm might, for instance, think that it's competing directly with big-name design firms for home remodeling jobs—when its most direct competition might be the free design consultations provided by chain home centers that also sell huge volumes of remodeling supplies.

## Case Study — Drivesavers

*Scott Gaidano is in the miracle business. Frantic business customers call him with tales of computer hard drives and servers that have suddenly gone haywire—maybe drowned by a cup of coffee or frazzled by a power surge. Drivesavers, Gaidano's California-based service, takes gummed-up hard drives and extracts the data that customers feared was gone forever.*

*For years, Gaidano had customers disassemble their machines, pull out the failed drive, and send it to his small plant via private delivery service. His staff would fix it and then return it via Federal Express. Often, the drives would spend more time in transit than they did actually being fixed.*

*Gaidano knew that some customers would pay a premium to get their restored data faster. He set up a secure portion of the company's web site (www.drivesavers.com) where his technicians could park the data from a rescued drive. The customer could then choose to download the data onto another (presumably functioning) computer in his or her office, or even through a remote location such as an office service center, for $50 more than the $275 minimum fee.*

*Not only was the remote-retrieval option a success with customers who tested it out, but Gaidano discovered that it solved a knotty problem for overseas customers as well—they no longer had to wait for the salvaged drives to clear customs upon re-entry into their countries.*

Think not only of competitors that are superficially similar to your company or belong to the same professional association, but also those that might be affiliated with other services, manufacturers and stores. A manufacturer of powdered finishes that are applied to metal parts and then fired for a shiny, impervious finish for cars and machinery might assume that his sales reps will be duking it out with other sales reps as they try to supply metal processing plants with various finishes. But the company might find that its most threatening competitor is a finishing shop that makes and applies its own brand of powdered finish—and that a new process designed to apply coatings to a finished end product is in the works.

You may want to marshal your data on industry trends and competitors' positions within your target market to see which distribution channels claim the most overall sales volume. You may detect an opportunity to distinguish yourself through an overlooked channel.

# SWOT ANALYSIS

Each distribution channel alternative and sales force option carries specific costs and advantages, as well as inherent disadvantages. Analyzing these **strengths, weaknesses, opportunities and threats (a SWOT analysis)** can provide you a thumbnail sketch of distribution channels that you can organize into a chart for quick comparison.

Drawing on your prior analysis of the market environment, ask yourself:

- What are the barriers (difficulties) to entering this product category via each distribution channel?

- How much do various distribution channels cost to successfully enter? Over what period of time is this money being spent?

- Should we distribute our business products locally, regionally or nationally? And in what order, or through all channels at the same time?

- Are some or all of the items we sell subject to varying product life cycles? How do our products compare to competitor product life cycles by channel?

- What types of competitive spending, promotions, advertising and field sales response will our business entry encounter by type of distribution channel?

- How hard and expensive is it to enter this product category? Might startup competitors suddenly crowd into your distribution channels?

- Is the geographic location of your customer a driving factor or irrelevant?

- What distribution channels are seasonal (such as an annual tradeshow)?

- What is the absolute size of key direct competitors and what financial resources and business partnerships and affiliations do they have to their advantage?

# COSTS OF DISTRIBUTION CHANNELS

As you consider different distribution channels, you'll soon realize that this decision will have a ripple effect on your packaging, product positioning, marketing strategy and administrative costs. It's rarely a simple matter of comparing, say, one retail store to another, or UPS vs. Federal Express. The puzzle pieces you'll have to fit together include:

- Would you rather pay more to completely control the distribution channel—such as buying your own trucks and hiring your own drivers—or engage a wholesaler or distributor, over which you'll have less control, but which will free you from sinking precious capital into creating your own channel?

- Will a completely unique distribution channel, such as your own line of boutiques, significantly add to your brand image?

- Is timely delivery more important than the price of delivery? Tax specialists command a premium for in-person consultations from January through April 15.

- Is price more important than timely delivery? If you simply want your office cleaned twice a week, you may be more than happy to settle for Tuesdays and Thursdays if the cleaning service offers you a 15 percent discount to take those unpopular slots in its calendar.

- How might you adjust the package and shipping container to minimize the cost of delivery?

- What work can you bring in-house that will cut the price? U.S. Post Office staffers can give you guidelines for presorting catalogs so that you cut the cost of bulk mail even more.

- How might you adapt emerging technologies to continually trim distribution charges, or even replace your current method with an altogether new one?

## Case Study — Geek Squad

*"Geek." To Robert Stephens, that's a compliment.*

*As president of the Minneapolis-based Geek Squad, Stephens has transformed the commonplace services of computer training and troubleshooting into a distinctive brand. Instead of adopting a glitzy logo and high-tech graphics for his platoon of technicians-on-the-spot, he decided to claim the "geek" label and transform it.*

*Stephens used 1950s gas-station logos as inspiration for the oval "Geek Squad" logo. The fedoras, black suits and narrow neckties that his employees wear were inspired by the old cop show* Dragnet. *He even retrofitted old ice cream trucks with Geek Squad logos so clients know exactly when their geek has arrived to fix their computers. (Embarrassed corporate clients can request an incognito arrival to spare their information technology departments the humiliation of being rescued by the Geek Squad.)*

*All this would just be so much gimmick if Stephens didn't have a rock-solid service under the flashy trash. He guarantees that all incoming calls are answered within seven minutes. Staffers are on-call, via beeper, on rotating shifts, 24 hours a day, 365 days a year. Though the $75 an hour fee seems steep, Stephens' proprietary manuals for nearly every configuration of hardware and software enable his staffers to diagnose and fix glitches quickly. Nevertheless, the $150 per hour off-hours emergency rate is growing in popularity.*

*Even as he's rolling out the Geek Squad to other Midwest cities (via strategically located branch offices), Stephens is making sure he can deliver by ramping up a Geek University for training scores of new employees.*

# Figuring Your Costs

Since your choice of distribution channels affects so many aspects of marketing and selling your product, you'll need to consider what that choice means to your bottom line. Each channel has a unique set of circumstances that must be accommodated and paid for:

1.  The staffer who manages distribution must be compensated, in addition to support staff, including portions of time devoted by customer service, sales support staffers, receptionists and others who will be handling inquiries about distribution.

2.  What advertising, promotion or other media will be used to support this distribution media? Do the design of the product, package and materials provided with the product dictate a particular type of distribution system or consideration (fragile, oversized, fancy tags that must be packed carefully, and so on).

3.  Will you use a broker? What commission or percentage of sales will he charge?

4.  Will you use a distributor/wholesaler? What discounts, for what volumes, will they expect? What additional fees will they charge (refrigeration, special handling and other considerations)?

5.  What packing materials and outside shipping container will you use? Can you adapt an off-the-shelf solution or must it be custom-made?

6.  What is the cost of shipping? How promptly does the customer expect the shipment to arrive? Does the nature of the product dictate a short, more costly, mode of shipping (as for seasonal or perishable goods)? Will you need insurance? Can you work with another supplier to this customer or distributor to pool shipments, and thereby gain lower rates?

7.  How will you confirm receipt of the shipment? Do customers expect to be able to check on the status of their order online via your web site? If so, what will it cost to install a system tracker, bar code software and printer, bar-code reader and other supporting technology?

8.  Does the final retailer require a slotting, placement, or other fee for placement on the shelf?

9.  Is it customary in your industry for retailers or distributors to return unsold goods for a refund? What percent of goods are typically returned, and for how much of a refund on the price paid by the retailer or distributor?

## Case Study — Distribution Options for House Salad Dressing

*Distribution, packaging and pricing are interdependent. Here are the considerations that a small Italian restaurant weighed before deciding how it might bottle and distribute its regionally famous house salad dressing.*

*The **first option** was simply to mix up extra batches of the dressing, pour it into some sterilized 32-ounce jars, and plunk it in a little display next to the cashier's counter with a sign reading "Our Famous House Dressing, $5." Distribution was only a matter of carrying the jars from the kitchen to the counter, so no shipping cost had to be figured in. Each 24 jars sold would yield a gross revenue of $120, or 15.625 cents per ounce.*

*Advantages to this scheme were its simplicity and the ability to produce only as much dressing as they seemed to be selling on a daily basis. Disadvantages were that the brand name wouldn't be extended outside the restaurant, or to consumers who'd never visited the restaurant. The dressing wouldn't do much to encourage new customers—packaging and selling it was mainly a service for existing customers.*

*The **second option** was to sell the dressing locally through specialty food stores. Because the owners had their hands full just running the restaurant, they'd have to hire a part-time sales rep to chat up the store owners, persuade them to take on the dressing, and make sure stock was constantly replenished.*

*Advantages to the second option were that the local stores were tolerant of the non-standard 32-ounce jar size, that the brand was extended beyond the confines of the restaurant, and that local purchasers wouldn't have to go too far out of their way to visit the restaurant. Disadvantages included the 10 percent fee that the sales rep took, plus the 10 percent distribution cost for the trucks and crates. Gross revenue was 12.5 cents per ounce.*

*The **third option** was to license production of the dressing to a local food processor who could produce the dressing in bulk. It would then have to be distributed in bulk, which meant that it would have to go in a more standard 26-ounce jar. A jar that retailed for $3.75 would cost $1.80 at wholesale. The distributor would take a 25 percent discount, resulting in a 5.2 cents per ounce gross revenue reverting back to the restaurant, after all was said and done.*

*Advantages to this option were the enormous boost to the brand that regional distribution would bring. It would be free advertising for the restaurant to have its salad dressing on the shelves of hundreds of grocery stores. And restaurant advertising could easily include a list of locations where the dressing was available. Establishing a relationship with a food processor could pave the way for bigger and better things—maybe a whole line of frozen food or an Italian bread topping. And the restaurant would still be making some money.*

*Disadvantages? Well, not many of those thousands of consumers who saw the bottles on the shelf would find it convenient to visit the restaurant. Many of those brand impressions would be wasted, as far as the restaurant was concerned. Maintaining relationships with the food processor, distributors, wholesalers and retailers could prove exhausting. It might take a long time to collect the money from the sales, and the bookkeeping was complicated. Quality of the dressing would have to be constantly monitored, considering that it was being produced out of sight of the restaurant. And if it was a hit, would rapid expansion of the brand undermine the restaurant owners' core commitment to their eatery?*

# Handling Returns

In a perfect world, every product that goes out the door or every service you perform will perfectly satisfy each and every customer. Unfortunately, some factors are out of your control, and even if you do everything right, sometimes you still may have an unhappy consumer. Maybe a product is damaged during delivery or goes unsold on a shelf during its useful life cycle. Or, for whatever reason, a customer misunderstands or is unhappy with a particular service.

You need to plan for these contingencies, and how you handle them may make the difference between a happy—and loyal—customer and one who chooses not to patronize you again.

1.  Will your return policy be a prominent element in your marketing strategy? What restrictions (time and place) and requirements (receipt, original packaging intact and so on) will you include in your return policy?

2.  Will you enact a "no questions asked' return policy, or will you, in fact, want to converse with dissatisfied customers about the reason for the return and related matters? If you'll want to talk with customers, how will you convey that expectation through packaging inserts, marketing support, online and other media?

3.  Will you have a returns form that customers must fill out? If not, how will you track the nature and reason for returns?

4.  Which staffers will process returns, and how much of their time will be devoted to that task?

5.  What are the industry norms as to the percentage of goods damaged in transit, returned or otherwise unsaleable, so that you can benchmark your distributors and make financial allowances for likely losses resulting from flawed distribution?

6.  What will you do with the returned material? Options include selling it in a semi-regular "garage" clearance; selling it through a clearance center or auctioning it off through your web site; selling it to an odd-lots jobber who will then sell it to retail bargain stores; donating it to charity (if it's in good working order); giving it to employees; refurbishing it and reselling it, labeled as such; and throwing it out.

# PRIORITIZING DISTRIBUTION OPTIONS

You might be able to launch your product or services in several channels simultaneously—but that's unlikely. More typically, small companies carefully choose the one or two most promising distribution channels and then measure their success. As your sales volume grows and your array of products or services broadens, you'll be able to experiment with additional methods of distribution.

Or, you may want to develop several parallel marketing campaigns for different distribution channels. If you're selling vitamins, you might first start out by selling to health food stores through company reps and sales brokers, and then take on a separate set of reps for mainstream grocery stores. You'll also have to evaluate the relative merits of multi-level marketing "networks," warehouse clubs, direct mail, individual distributors, and affiliations with traditional or alternative medical and therapeutic practitioners.

In any event, you'll be constantly evaluating the efficacy of your distribution channels. Measure their value by asking:

- What are the financial resources and risks of this channel? Do downstream vendors pay their bills promptly? Can you develop a relationship with them, or are they likely to dump your line for a competing one that offers a penny or two more of profit?

- How do your distributors cooperate with you—reinforcing marketing plans and helping you evaluate the market and new product ideas?

- What are competitors' strengths and market share? Might they buy one of the main industry distributors, or do they have so much clout that the distributor might enact policies to placate them while putting you at a disadvantage?

- What is your management experience with each type of channel?

- How does this channel enhance your product positioning with target buyers? Does the channel make it easy and convenient for your target buyers to acquire your goods or services?

# Chapter 8

# Sales and
# Customer Relations

Real salesmen don't wear plaid.

This comes as a relief to many entrepreneurs. In particular, those who have spent most of their careers in medium sized or large companies may never have had much to do with real, live salespeople. Sales was accomplished by "them"—outgoing, competitive folks, always on the road, enjoying lush expense accounts and bragging about their juicy commissions.

Now that you're building your own business, you've become one of "them." Fortunately, the most effective salespeople are those who genuinely believe that they're helping their clients through the products or services that they represent. Without being condescending, they truly want their prospects to understand how the product or service will make their business or personal life easier, or will help them achieve a business or personal goal. That heartfelt enthusiasm not only comes through in person, but it also buoys good salespeople through the inevitable bouts of rejection.

You believe in your company's mission statement and in the unique attributes of your product or service. You wouldn't be going through all this work if you didn't believe you could make a genuine improvement in the lives of your customers or clients. Now it's time to put your knowledge of market trends; analysis of competitors; and carefully designed pricing, packaging and distribution structures all together into a coherent sales plan. With that plan, you'll be equipped to go out and meet the potential customers that you've been researching.

# YOUR SALES PHILOSOPHY

Few entrepreneurs intend to deceive or disappoint their customers. Yet, how many times have you felt, as a customer, that the retailer or service company you purchased from didn't give a darn about the transaction or even care if you ever returned? Balancing your company's revenue and other goals with your desire to steadily build a base of satisfied, repeat customers is tricky. With apologies to legendary Victorian Chicago retailer Marshall Field, the customer isn't always right—just almost always. With some forethought, you can develop a strategy that will enable to you serve your customers fairly and profitably.

What kind of relationship do you want to have with your customers? Do you want them to see you as a premium-priced supplier that's always likely to have what they need readily available? Or are your customers willing to sacrifice selection for low price and moderate quality? How will you encourage customers to return for additional sales—because of personal service, your price guarantee, convenience, or your custom-produced product or service?

Essentially, your sales philosophy is simply your brand positioning statement *from your customer's point of view*. You might or might not post your sales philosophy where your customers can read it, but every person in your company should consider it a daily credo. It's the yardstick against which every customer interaction is measured.

An auto tire repair and replacement service, for instance, might adopt this sales philosophy: "We pledge to serve our customers politely, efficiently and honestly. Our goal is to fix every problem within six hours." With such an explicit sales philosophy, every employee has a clear idea of how they're to treat customers. Palming off used tires as new is verboten. So is taking a half-hour coffee break just as three customers limp in with flat tires.

## You Are Your Own Best Salesperson

Though the thought of making sales calls may make you quake in your boots, you have one advantage that no one else in the world does: You are the owner of your company. No one can understand the benefits of your services and products better than you. Buyers frequently prefer to deal with company owners because they know that they've got the one person who can't pass the buck. You're the final authority on whether that negotiated price is OK or whether you can deliver that research report in just four weeks.

## Case Study — Joel Baumwoll Consulting

*Consultant Joel Baumwoll is a guy with a golden Rolodex. He follows up every successful project with a thank-you note and a request for a short note commenting on his services and endorsing him. That gives him an arsenal of ready-made professional character witnesses whom he can quote on his web site, in sales letters and in marketing materials.*

*When Baumwoll identifies a company to which he'd like to offer his consulting services, he calls acquaintances whom he figures have contacts in the appropriate departments within that company. Once he's got the right name, he doesn't hesitate to drop the name of the recommender in his introductory letter. "I can say honestly that so-and-so suggested that I call," he says.*

*Chances are that his new prospects have already heard of Baumwoll. His broader marketing strategy relies heavily on regularly writing opinion and analysis articles about his specialty—positioning brands—for a select group of trade magazines. Not only do the articles bolster Baumwoll's credibility among his peers, current clients and future prospects, but the reprints (made with permission, of course) are also great marketing materials to give prospects during sales calls.*

Leverage this advantage shamelessly. Business executives often prefer to deal with those who are at least their peers, so aim high. Don't settle for an hour pitching a junior assistant purchasing clerk when you could be getting to know the senior operations manager.

Be sure that you've done your homework before you approach a new prospect. Research the company, its growth record, its strengths and its weaknesses, so you can figure out exactly why and how your product or service will help it grow.

Your most powerful sales device is your ability to listen to your potential customer and understand his goals and aspirations. Strive to establish a partnership approach from the beginning by concentrating on listening to your customer instead of nervously rattling off a laundry list of what your company does. Your company's offerings are only relevant to your potential customer if they help him achieve his goals.

## It Worked for Them!

*The owner of a chain of furniture stores was having a hard time getting sales clerks to approach and talk with customers. Customers didn't want to feel pressured by a pushy clerk, yet still wanted to have clerks within shouting distance to answer questions. The solution: a fun quiz on "How to discover your unique decorating style" that the clerks gave browsers.*

*That's irresistible—who wouldn't want to know if they fell in the "innovator" or "nestor" or another category? Customers enjoyed spending a few minutes answering questions about their decorating preferences and clerks could break the ice by discussing the quiz results with customers.*

Making the transition from small talk to selling can be smooth if you follow these classic steps:

- First, discuss the prospect's goals and expectations for the type of product or service that you offer. What does he or she want to achieve?

- Then, discuss the specifics of the customer's situation and the most important factors that will determine the purchase choice. These could be price, convenience, specific functions of the product, reliability or other factors.

- Develop a plan that incorporates the benefits of your product or service with action that the customer can take to achieve the desired end.

- Confirm that the customer wants to consummate the purchase. Either work on the contract on the spot or negotiate the specifics and prepare to deliver the completed contract as soon as possible.

## Work Smart

*Cold calling is intimidating, no doubt about it. Warm calling, though, is considerably easier—and hot calling is the best of all.*

*Simply calling potential customers can be awkward. It often helps to break the ice non-verbally—perhaps by sending a humorous postcard, bouquet of flowers, or half of a product prototype or intriguing report summary. When you follow up a few days later, you're not simply asking, "Did you get my introductory letter," but "Did you enjoy the flowers?" or "Would you like to see the other half of that prototype or report summary?" You've got a ready-made conversation starter.*

*Develop a three-minute script that introduces yourself, mentions your company name, and states the specific reason why you're calling. At this point, you're not asking for the sale, but for permission to tell the prospect more. You might offer to send a brochure, product sample, or set up a time to drop by for a brief demo or discussion. Be sure to respect the prospect's time by keeping your initial call brief.*

*Now your first person-to-person meeting is with a **warm prospect**. Be sure you've got all the relevant information in hand—pricing, delivery mode and timing, and, most importantly, what your product or service will do to further your customer's own business or personal goals.*

*Often, inexperienced salespeople are so relieved to actually have a meeting that they rush ahead with a laundry list of product attributes and completely neglect to ask their prospect about their own business or personal needs. "Tell me a little about your company and where you're headed" is an open-ended question that signals your desire to help your prospect accomplish his goals— and, of course, you'll also pick up valuable information as you listen.*

*Fearlessly ask about what pleases and frustrates your prospect about products or services already available in your sales category. He may surprise you by pointing out key weaknesses of your competitors that you had been wondering how to exploit. If he says, "I'm happy with my current supplier," you might ask, "What would your ideal deal for this product or service look like?" You may hear about an unrequited hope that you can fulfill.*

*Even as you're telling your prospect about your offering (stressing benefits at all times), be sure to ask lots of questions along the way. Keep your prospect engaged in the discussion; someone who's agreeing with you that, yes, this new package is far safer for caustic chemicals than your competitor's is someone who's warming up indeed.*

*A **hot prospect** is someone who has already decided, through their own diagnosis or by paying attention to your advertising, promotions and media coverage, that they're quite interested in your product or service. Even if someone appears ready to sign on the dotted line as soon as you enter the office, be sure to make sure the prospect understands the benefits and attributes of your product or service anyway. Enthusiasm is no substitute for knowledge.*

Of course, you're not just plumping for any old prospect. You want to spend your time and effort on the most *qualified* prospects. A qualified prospect:

- fits the demographic and lifestyle, or business, profile of your target market

- knows enough about your product or service category (and his own) to understand the terminology you'll be using and how the benefits you're pointing out are of value to the company

- has the authority and autonomy to approve a purchase

- has the authority to ensure that the purchase will be completed—i.e., that the software will be installed or the clothes actually put on the rack

- has access to the company's financial reports and records so that he or she will be able to trace the impact of your product or service on his company.

Once you've established your criteria for your short list of qualified sales prospects, it's time to compile a list of who they are. You, or an assistant, can cull your market research for companies or categories of consumers that appear to have the strongest need or desire for what you're selling. Once you know who they are, you can decide how you'll approach them. Classic approaches include direct contact, such as through personal sales calls, a retail location or direct mail; telemarketing; or electronic direct marketing.

## Potential Pitfall

*Even a well-qualified prospect may not be able to sign off on a large purchase without involving others. Bosses, peers and subordinates all may have a say in the type, price and style of product or service that's finally approved, and you may end up developing relationships with them as well as the primary purchaser.*

*Don't overlook administrative staffers, either; by being cheerful and polite to your prospect's secretary (even while being told that "The boss is, um, still in a meeting.") you'll gain this person's respect—and those impressions, good or bad, will probably be passed on to the boss.*

# Sales Materials

No matter how you choose to sell, you'll need to have a well-thought-through approach that integrates personal contact with follow-through material. This is where all your careful preparation in researching your market, your target customers, and your competition converges. Your sales materials need to provide a sense of company purpose and direction, as well as clear explanations of exactly what services or products you offer.

Specific benefits to the particular prospect you're addressing might be outlined in your cover letter, particularly if you do only custom work, such as creating prototype machine parts. If the benefits of your product are about the same for a significant number of prospects, then it probably is worthwhile to develop a glossy printed piece targeted just for them.

If, for instance, you're a small business computer consultant who specializes in local and wide area networking, the benefits to most prospective customers are about the same: namely, the ability to integrate client-server technology into their operations, to enable employees to communicate seamlessly, to store data on a centrally accessible server, and to smoothly access the Internet. Those universal points can be made in a special piece, with your cover letter tailoring your sales pitch even more specifically to the goals that particular prospect has for networking the office.

It's often a good idea to produce various elements of your sales support material as stand-alone pieces. That way, you can mix and match materials in the package to suit the needs of each potential client. As well, you can easily add new and updated sheets, without the expense of printing an entirely new set of material. Sales materials can include:

- an introductory brochure that simply outlines your company, what it does, how it benefits customers, and how to contact you. Wording and graphics on the brochure should be as timeless as possible so that you can use it for many purposes. Many companies make this core piece as nice-looking as possible to make a strong first impression. Professionally produced graphics, pictures and four-color printing will go a long way toward making a favorable impression.

- a folder (usually custom-printed with your company colors and logo) with a die-cut interior slot to hold business cards. Individually printed sales pieces can be inserted, along with the company brochure and cover letter, to reflect the specific services or products of interest to that prospect.

- a sheet that outlines the range of products or services you offer. If they work together in some way—say, if you sell electronic pagers and also monthly pager service—explain how.

- individual product or service sheets that include pictures, technical specifications, and very specific features and benefits.

- a company bio sheet that includes a one- or two-paragraph company history and mission statement, as well as very brief introductions to the key executives and their professional backgrounds.

- testimonials or case studies of current customers and how your products and services benefited them.

- leave-behinds—such as research reports, an overview of the charts and statistics included in a presentation you've given, or worksheets—that prospects can review at their leisure. Don't forget to staple another of your business cards to these.

Some of this material can be delivered electronically through your company web site. Set up a password-protected section just for prospective customers. Give them the password at the end of your meeting and urge them to explore the site. Explain that the password is only valid for however long you've determined—usually about a month. Include in the site interactive elements, such as worksheets and calculators, that can help prospects figure out the direct benefit to them of your products and services. You might also include lengthier testimonials, samples of work you've recently completed for other customers, and samples of materials or information that's included in your ongoing customer service effort, such as your latest customer newsletter.

Price sheets are usually printed as needed, both to reflect current prices and availability. That can easily be done in-house with a standard word processing program and high-quality printer. The more customized the product or service is, the less appropriate it is to present pricing material as a matter of course to prospects. Not only do you want them to completely understand the product or service and see how it can directly benefit them before they're distracted by price, but semi-custom and custom products and services are, by definition, created specifically to fit that particular customer's needs. You can't quote a project price until you understand the scope of the project—which you accomplish by discussing the customer's goals with him or her.

Some prospects will push for a range of prices early on to see if the figure they have in mind is at all consistent with what you might charge. Think ahead of time about how you'll handle that kind of question. You might come up with a prototype example that outlines how you charged one client, what the client got, and what the client's direct return on investment for the purchase was. Don't just hand it over to your prospects—carefully walk through each point and be sure they understand that pricing for their project would be determined by their own needs.

## Successful Sales Presentations

Once you've got that hot, qualified prospect interested in hearing more about your product or service, what do you do next?

Set up a time to talk in person. And then prepare, prepare, prepare. Find out:

- Has your prospect company ever bought this sort of product before? If so, were they satisfied with their experience? If they were satisfied with the experience, why are they thinking about switching suppliers? Price, customer service, the ability of the supplier to continue to support the account, or other factors? Ask yourself: If the target is already pre-sold on the concept of the product or service you offer, how will you respond to questions about your company's particular services, pricing and ability to consistently deliver?

- If the prospect has never before bought this type of product, what kind of introductory material should you have ready either to discuss at the meeting or to leave behind?

- What might be several ultimate goals that your prospect has in mind for using your product or service? Get a bead on what kind of competitive market your prospect is facing so that you can point out how the benefits of your product or service specifically will help achieve that goal.

- Are there any suppliers or others who have regular dealings with your prospect who might give you some insight as to how this person prefers to run meetings and makes decisions? Some people like to shoot the breeze about the latest pro hockey playoffs and the likelihood of a late spring shower before they ease into the real reason for the sales call. Others want you to just list the benefits, the cost, and what your qualifications are. Of course, you'll be looking for these clues from the moment you shake the prospect's hand, but any early insight you can gain will give you confidence that you're getting started on the right foot.

- Consider the type of information that you'll probably be presenting. Start by outlining the problem or aspiration that the prospect has that you can help solve or achieve. Often, it helps to have some specific statistics and facts about market trends to give context and credibility to the problem or aspiration.

- Then, move into a discussion of specifically how your product or service solves the problem or equips the prospect to reach the aspiration. Yes, talk about the features your product or service offers—but only in the context of the benefits that directly help the prospect.

- Answer the prospect's questions. This is best done by carefully listening to the prospect's comments and questions. Don't get so carried away by your wonderfully constructed presentation that you forget to answer questions as they arise.

- Technological tools, such as computer-aided charts and dancing graphs, can work for you or against you. Be sure you have fully mastered the technology—practice, practice, practice. Check well in advance to see if the room in which you're making your presentation can accommodate the notebook computer, projector, screen and any other accoutrements. If your presentation involves referring to a web site, capture the screens on disc ahead of time and integrate them into your presentation—don't count on going online in the middle of the meeting. Finally, be sure you, not your technology, drives the meeting. Your computer does not want to develop a mutually profitable relationship with the prospect—you do. It's better to have a low-tech presentation than a high-tech one that distracts from your message.

- If the prospect states objections or disagrees, don't get defensive. Ask this person to tell you more about how he came to that conclusion. The prospect may be misunderstanding what your company does, your qualifications, or some other aspect of what you're about. Or he may have zeroed-in on a legitimate point that you'd overlooked. If so, graciously concede the point and promise to present a full answer within a day or two. (And then, do.)

- Your goal is to have the prospect agree with you that the problem or aspiration exists, that it's one that the prospect wants or needs to solve, and that you are the person to present that solution.

- Once you're at that point, know how you will confirm the sale. It might be through a proposal outlining what you're going to do with or for the client, a sales contract, or another form of closing the sale. Be sure that payment policies are clearly understood, too.

(source: Power Presentations, Chicago, pwerpres@interaccess.com)

## It Worked for Them!

 *Larry Novick has plenty of services to offer clients—investment advice, taxes, accounting. But the president of Fiducial TripleCheck doesn't just launch into his menu of offerings when he meets a prospective new client. He usually lets the client set the pace by coming to him with a request for a particular service—then cross-sells the client on additional services once TripleCheck has successfully completed one assignment.*

*Though it's low glamour, income tax preparation is a huge driver for TripleCheck. More and more people are reluctant to handle their taxes on their own—and, of course, small business owners and people with complicated investments and assets are also likely to need additional financial services.*

*"If they trust you enough to open up to give you information from their tax return, you know right away that they need financial services," says Novick. "They've already built up that trust relationship."*

*As his staffers work on clients' tax returns, they keep notes on the life stage that the clients are in, how they tend to save and spend money, and what financial needs may be on the horizon.*

*With all that information available, it's a simple matter to ask a client in the last tax consultation "What are you doing for retirement?" or "How are you preparing for your children's college educations?"*

*Sometimes, clients are in the happy position of receiving a large tax refund that they can immediately apply to savings and investments goals—that Novick's staff helps them shape.*

*Clients find out about TripleCheck through the 8 x 4-inch ads that Novick runs in local newspapers every week. Typically, each ad has a newsy headline and is followed by a short article explaining some new financial term or a portion of new financial legislation. Local residents hear Novick interview other experts every Saturday morning in a radio show he hosts on financial topics. As well, Novick courts newcomers to his area by sending letters to new homeowners explaining some of the latest twists in homeowners' tax rules and inviting them to come into his office for a free consultation.*

# Getting Sales Help

While every company CEO needs to be able to smoothly present his company's mission at the drop of a hat, you may nevertheless find that sales just isn't your cup of tea. If that's so, you'll want to hire a sales manager to initially sell for you, and then hire, train and supervise a network of sales reps.

While good salespeople love to keep score with a variety of methods—annual revenues, percentage of increase over the prior period, winning over a competitor's customer—be sure that you aren't so wowed by a sales manager candidate's personal victories that you forget that you really are hiring him to develop the entire sales side of your company. He or she also needs to be a team player, willing to share commissions and credit with sales assistants and customer support staffers. A good sales manger needs to be flexible to adapt his sales approach to various sub-markets, and to be enthusiastic about training, for his own sake and to lead the reps.

You'll need to work with your sales manager to determine how you should develop your sales organization. Do you need:

- salespeople for one-on-one sales?

- sales reps who represent your product or service along with those of non-competing companies in the same product category?

- salespeople who are comfortable handling a sale from initial contact through the last detail of customer service?

- salespeople who aren't threatened by integrating technology into their jobs?

- telemarketers who can ply the phones and play the game of odds that they'll be able to better the typical 1 to 2 percent response rate?

- telemarketers who only receive incoming calls generated by consumer response to direct mail pieces, catalogs or other modes of advertising?

## Case Study — Stratamar, Inc.

*Especially when you're just starting out, it's easy to get immersed in one client's project and let the rest of your marketing and sales goals slide. Neil Brown, president of Stratamar, Inc., a sports marketing advisory firm in Ohio, found this out the hard way. He found that the ebb and flow of his business is more like a semi-annual high and low tide. Though he tried to doggedly keep up with making new contacts and developing new proposals even while meeting deadlines for current clients, he often let sales efforts languish while he cranked out a knockout project.*

*Brown learned his lesson when he became so wrapped up in a client's startup that he neglected marketing for six whole months. When the client abruptly pulled the plug on the startup, Brown was left high and dry. He struggled for three months before enough new work was rolling in to keep Stratamar afloat.*

*Now, Brown has himself on a strict sales contact schedule. He blocks out time in his calendar to meet new people, cultivate new prospects, sharpen his presentation skills and pitch new projects. To keep him on the straight and narrow, he has a couple of trusted friends and his wife periodically ask him how he's keeping up with his sales efforts.*

# E-Commerce Sales

Could you cut costs and improve customer satisfaction simultaneously by selling directly through your web site? To find out, ask yourself:

- How would that affect your relationship with current customers/distribution chain, even suppliers?

- What additional benefit will customers get by buying through a web site?

- Will you be able to unload overstocks, returned merchandise and other materials through a site, without competing with current customers?

- Are your customers so price-sensitive that they would value constant price updates on that web site?

- Do you have the resources to design, install and devote staff to maintaining the web site and orders that come in through it?

- Are your customers sufficiently web-savvy that they will quickly understand how to use your site?

- Will the site open up additional markets (outside your immediate geography, via links with related sites, etc.) that couldn't happen in the "real" world?

You may or may not make money from your e-commerce effort. Consider not just the amount of sales you gain from the site, but other, less tangible benefits, such as reducing response time to customer questions by a third, or saving time and hassle by posting old press releases so reporters can look them up online instead of having staff dig out backgrounders and mail or fax them.

If you do decide to proceed with the site, start with the least-risky functions, and keep "real world" duplications so that customers aren't left hanging. Gradually move into mission-critical functions, but only after you've thoroughly tested the use of your e-commerce system and internal staff support, and asked your customers how it's working out for them.

# CUSTOMER SERVICE

In a way, a completed transaction with a customer is more a beginning than an end—the beginning of a continuing, (hopefully) mutually beneficial relationship. The rule of thumb is that it costs five to eight times more to obtain a new customer than it does to sell again to an existing customer.

Not only do current customers represent numerous opportunities for additional sales, but they may also refer new customers or clients to you, help spread the word about the benefits of your company's products or services, and even help you test new products and services. *Customer service is internal marketing for future sales from existing customers.*

## Continuing the Dialogue

An ongoing dialogue with customers is invaluable to your company's growth. As the pace of technological change continues to increase, your customers can serve as a crucial early warning system; they may be able to help you pinpoint new products, services, delivery systems or other innovations that can boost your sales and help you gain market share. They may also help you understand how their needs and aspirations are affected by market trends and technology, which in turn will help you shape and present new products or services. In short, they can be informal partners that help you stay proactive (ahead of the trends) rather than reactive (always trying to catch up).

Post-sales dialogue with your customers completes the communications loop that's started with a successful sale. One popular and effective way of encouraging the repetition of this loop is through the use of company newsletters. In addition, newsletters also serve as useful marketing materials when mining for new customers— offering proof of your ability to satisfy other customers.

# Sample Newsletter

*Whether it's print, e-mail, web or fax, customers and clients often appreciate regular updates on what's happening with your company—that can benefit them. Useful copy includes brief highlights of studies you've done, news trends, new product introductions, and tips for getting more from your products and services. Updates can take the form of:*

- *print newsletters sent out on a regular schedule, at least quarterly*
- *a section of your web site accessible through the site and through e-mails sent directly to customers*
- *oversized postcards with just one or two short articles printed on them*
- *a fax or e-mail newsletter with simple graphics and one or two brief articles and several news and tips items*

*Brody Communications Ltd., a small consulting firm that advises corporations and individuals on etiquette, presentation and speech coaching, and personal communication skills, sends out a quarterly newsletter called "Keynotes." Clients depend on receiving it to remind them to schedule seminars and to order products—but it's far more than a direct-mail vehicle. By providing at least two how-to articles in each issue, anyone who reads it will get ideas that they can immediately use to groom their own communications skills. In effect, the newsletter is a bit of sampling device because readers get to try out the recommendations made by Marjorie Brody, the firm's owner, in her presentations and materials.*

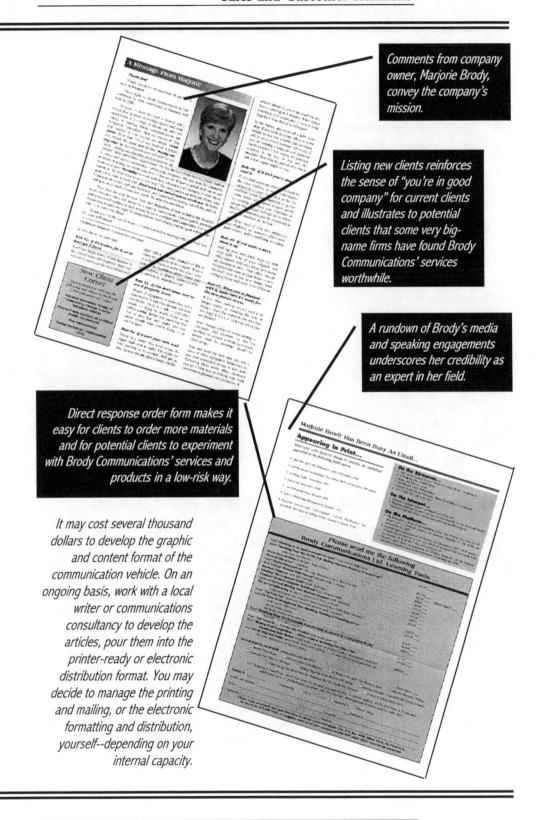

Comments from company owner, Marjorie Brody, convey the company's mission.

Listing new clients reinforces the sense of "you're in good company" for current clients and illustrates to potential clients that some very big-name firms have found Brody Communications' services worthwhile.

A rundown of Brody's media and speaking engagements underscores her credibility as an expert in her field.

Direct response order form makes it easy for clients to order more materials and for potential clients to experiment with Brody Communications' services and products in a low-risk way.

It may cost several thousand dollars to develop the graphic and content format of the communication vehicle. On an ongoing basis, work with a local writer or communications consultancy to develop the articles, pour them into the printer-ready or electronic distribution format. You may decide to manage the printing and mailing, or the electronic formatting and distribution, yourself--depending on your internal capacity.

## Work Smart

*Leverage the convenience and economy of electronic communications to produce an e-mail customer service newsletter. Like a print newsletter, an electronic newsletter needs to include information that's inherently useful to current and potential customers. Simply reiterating a sales pitch will only turn people off.*

*Genuinely useful information might include a roundup of recently released industry statistics (such as growth levels, as reported by an industry association); a preview of new thoughts, tips and ways to use your products and services that you may soon be formalizing with a new brochure or customer bulletin; very brief introductions of new key executives and their contact information; and short profiles of customers and how they've used your products or services to satisfy their customers and make their operations more profitable.*

*To be sure, some material from your print newsletter can be "repurposed" for an electronic version. However, people tend to read online material differently than they do print. Generally, items presented in an online format are shorter—no longer than 300 words for an article. Work with an experienced online media designer to come up with a format that's easily scanned by readers, and to develop an online archive of articles that can reside on your web site.*

*Keep in mind that your readers will have widely varying tolerances for fancy graphics and long download times. Though it's certainly possible to scan in product pictures, diagrams and other illustrations, it's probably better to save those for your web site. Your newsletter shouldn't be time-consuming and tedious to access, especially as it's dropped into readers' electronic mailboxes. Include your logo—perhaps in a simplified version—but otherwise keep the graphics bright, simple and minimal. And, don't forget to include a hyperlink to your company's web site.*

# Customer Management or Product Management?

It's easy to become so wrapped up in the business of running your business that you lose touch with your customers. Be on your guard for evidence that you're focusing so completely on your products or process that you're not really listening to your customers. One way to avoid this syndrome is to make quality and customer satisfaction a top priority for *all* employees in your company. As the owner of your company, you're in the best position to constantly reinforce the importance of customer service. Here are some steps to take.

1. **Quality work and customer satisfaction** must be a commitment of all employees. Personnel in *all jobs* must understand and commit to the Total Quality Management (TQM) program and work as a team. Every employee is in a position to make a difference to customers. Fork-lift operators can make recommendations that will streamline inventory management and order fulfillment. Receptionists are often overlooked, but the manner in which they answer the phone, how quickly they can find the right person to

answer the caller's question, and how graciously they receive visitors create indelible impressions. Create a company culture that encourages people to work creatively to assist customers—and be sure you recognize them for it!

2.  **Every company activity** must incorporate quality and customer satisfaction, including all communications with customers and suppliers. The more everyone in your company knows about your customer's business, needs, complaints and sources of satisfaction with your company, the more motivated, productive and efficient they will be. A billing clerk, for instance, may be able to recommend efficiencies eliminating layers of paperwork for a client.

3.  **It doesn't have to cost more** to make quality and customer satisfaction your priority. Creativity and timeliness, as well as frequent, consistent, truthful communication with each other and customers, go a long way. Encourage employees to work together across functional and departmental lines to solve problems.

4.  **Significant changes may be required** to make quality and customer satisfaction improvements. If employees are hesitant about making suggestions, researching their ideas and having their supervisors take them seriously, or if they believe that their initiatives will be nixed or get stalled by higher-ups in the company, they're unlikely to bother bringing up their ideas. If you ask for input and are met with a deafening silence, you may have to embrace a corporate cultural change, with quality and customer satisfaction as one of several major objectives.

5.  **Small advantages** in each company function can add up to a distinguishing difference in your marketplace. After all, would you rather pick up dinner at a pizzeria that packs your food in an insulated paper container and then a moisture-proof plastic bag, or one that simply slings the hot food in a flimsy paper bag?

6.  **Hire new employees** who are quality- and team-oriented.

7.  **Regularly seek customer feedback**. It is not enough to be satisfied that your business is doing a better job with its customers than the competition. The customers must also think so, providing at least quarterly feedback on company suppliers.

8.  **Choose suppliers that are committed to quality** so that you are working in sync with them, instead of trying to compensate for their mistakes and lackadaisical quality.

# Framing a Total Quality Management Program

These are some of the steps to take to build a successful TQM program:

- Provide specific programs, written guidelines and training sessions for all company personnel.

- Allow for decision-making and mistakes by all personnel.

- Provide a specific timetable for training, behavioral modification and feedback.

- Follow-up with customers to obtain feedback on the success of the new TQM programs.

- Commit to weeding out uncooperative company personnel.

- Be willing to visibly change, yourself; others will follow suit.

## Customer Service Action Forms

Use the following form to help create your own internal company customer satisfaction information and action sheet. Customize it to reflect the types of products and/or services that you offer. Consider carefully both the routing of the form through the company and when you should personally get involved. Hopefully, your employees should be able to handle many situations without involving you directly.

For example, if you deal in merchandise and the wrong items are shipped, your employees can quickly ship the right goods and arrange for a pick-up of the erroneous order. But if the goods are custom-made, or if it's your biggest customer, you might want to be part of the problem resolution process from the outset. And you'll want to have the form routed to you last. That way, you can review the types of issues being raised and see how your employees have resolved them.

Make it clear to your employees that this form isn't just window dressing: It is an important part of your business' efforts to satisfy your customers. Every employee should have a supply of these to get the ball rolling when faced with a situation that he or she cannot resolve. And everyone should be aware of the priority that these reports should be afforded and the turn-around time expected for resolution. Consider printing them on a distinctively colored paper so that they don't get lost on a desk or in an in-basket.

This type of form helps prevent customer problems from falling through the cracks, while at the same time providing for an orderly hand-off to someone who can address the matter. It also sends a couple of messages to your employees. First, there is a clear procedure to follow when a customer is unhappy. Second, you are looking to their good judgment to recognize problems and promptly suggest (and, frequently, implement) solutions. Third, it reinforces the message that your employees are a team, working to achieve common goals. In a well-run business, employees who are the primary customer contacts will originate many of these forms, not management.

| **Customer Service Action Form** | |
|---|---|
| Customer | Time & Date |
| | Originator |
| Telephone | Department |
| | Telephone |
| Situation requiring action | |
| **ROUTING** | |
| To | Department |
| Time received | |
| Action taken | |
| Recommended next steps | |
| To | Department |
| Time received | |
| Action taken | |
| Recommended next steps | |
| To | (last) |

# Leveraging Feedback from Customers

To be sure, you'll hear from some squeaky-wheel customers when something—anything—is wrong. Be careful to not generalize their experiences to your entire customer base. Many other clients or customers may have vague or specific dissatisfactions that they hesitate to mention. Perhaps they're embarrassed, or it feels like less work to gradually drift over to one of your competitors than it does to confront your sales rep or other company contact.

Finesse feedback from your entire customer base regularly—either on a set schedule or in the wake of a large project or intense selling season.

- Create a feedback form that's automatically sent to customers within a few days of each order or the completion of a project. Include a self-addressed envelope to improve the response rate. Ask for feedback on customers' general treatment by your employees and their impressions of your company, as well as details on their level of satisfaction and suggestions regarding their recent purchase. *And make sure all feedback comes directly to you. You don't want anyone filtering out or editing these responses. You need to see them all first.*

- Especially important suppliers may want to be in on your development of new products and services. Solicit their advice and insights as you shape new offerings.

- Compose and make widely available in your company a one-page customer satisfaction report that employees can use to document problems, complaints, suggestions and compliments as they occur. Be sure that supervisors circulate, discuss and act on patterns that they detect via the feedback forms. You may also want to post a "kudos and brickbats" bulletin board on your corporate Intranet.

- No feedback is worth the paper it's written on if top managers don't take it seriously. Be sure department managers know they're responsible for summarizing to you all customer comments and, when necessary, their responses to the customers. Once customers and employees know that you are interested in feedback, your company must act on what they say, and then provide status reports or presentations on the successful disposition of each problem or opportunity.

- Be sure to communicate to employees at large all success stories of problems solved, annoyed customers handled gracefully and lost customers regained. You can do this through a regular report memo, newsletter, broadcast e-mails or through your company newsletter or Intranet.

## Work Smart

*Give customers blanket permission to comment on the job your company's doing for them by formulating a Customer Bill of Rights. It might be a version of your sales philosophy or it might list very specific promises, such as "We pledge to complete your cleaning job within the estimated time—or the additional expense is on us."*

*Some companies post their bill of rights prominently in their customer sales departments, web sites, catalogs and other customer communications tools.*

## Customer Satisfaction Surveys

Customer satisfaction is the key to success. You want customers to be happy with the products and services you provide. If they feel they have received good value for their money, your business will prosper. Getting your customers to tell you what's good about your business, and where you need improvement, helps you to be sure that your business measures up to their expectations.

A customer satisfaction survey is one way to gather this vital information. There are any number of ways to get copies to your customers. Copies can be included with orders, mailed directly at regular intervals, sent and received by fax, whatever is convenient for your particular business. Many won't be returned, but those that are will make it worth your while.

The customer satisfaction survey nearby is designed to get your customers to tell you what they really think. No ranking of quality on a scale of one to five, no lengthy questions, just a list of key business activities and space to respond. Limiting the choices to "Outstanding" and "Needs Improvement" sends a clear message that you expect the products and service you supply to be the best available, period. Keeping the survey to a single page makes it more likely that customers will take the time to respond. It also facilitates faxing. Be sure to include instructions on how to return the completed surveys. Give your fax number, include self-addressed stamped envelopes, or whatever it takes to make it more likely that you'll get them back.

Don't forget to follow up on the comments you receive. If you have to change a procedure, tell an employee how you want things done, pick a new delivery service, do it. And advertise the fact that you did. Send thank-you notes to the customers whose comments caused you to make a change. Let them know that you can do an even better job because they took the time to help you improve.

## Sample Customer Satisfaction Survey
[print on company letterhead]

*We are constantly looking for ways to improve the quality of our products and services. To do that, we need to know what you think. We'd really appreciate it if you would take just a few minutes to respond to the handful of questions below. As a valued customer, how you rate our work is the most important information we can get.  Please help us do the job you deserve—the best possible!*

*Please return this survey [describe how you want the survey returned.]*

*Please circle "Outstanding" or "Needs Improvement" and comment:*

<u>**Products:**</u>                    *Outstanding*            *Needs Improvement*

_____

_____

_____

<u>**Services and Support:**</u>        *Outstanding*             *Needs Improvement*

_____

_____

_____

<u>**Delivery:**</u>                     *Outstanding*            *Needs Improvement*

_____

_____

_____

<u>**Ordering and Billing:**</u>       *Outstanding*             *Needs Improvement*

_____

_____

_____

<u>**Employees:**</u>                  *Outstanding*            *Needs Improvement*

_____

_____

_____

### Quality Improvement Exercise

*Every company, regardless of size, can improve quality and customer service. A simple exercise to improve quality is to track an order from its inception to final delivery. Try this list and see if any improvements can be made:*

*How are products and services sold (with what materials)?* _____
_____

*How and by whom is the order obtained from your customer?* _____
_____

*How is the order recorded for your company and your customer?* _____
_____

*How is the order processed within your company?* _____
_____

*Is there a system to check for any order discounts to customers?* _____
_____

*How long does it take to process and deliver the order to the customer?* _____
_____

*Do you have any accuracy checks for the order, with the customer and internally?* _____
_____

*How is the final product or service delivered to your customer?* _____
_____

*Have you checked customer relationship "manners" with everyone who has direct contact with your customers?* _____
_____

*Have you allowed everyone associated with order processing to meet periodically and discuss improvement possibilities?* _____
_____

*Do you have a customer follow-up procedure for orders?* _____
_____

# E-Commerce Customer Service

Customer service **online** combines many elements of classic good customer service with some new twists. Because your web site may be quite new to potential customers, you'll want to do everything you can to reassure them that their order is safe with you. Prominently post your privacy policy on your site, and check your ordering process regularly to be sure that it's as secure as you believe it is.

Though consumers and businesses are rapidly getting up to speed on buying via the Internet, it's still comforting to know that there's a real, live person (and a legitimate company) behind the site. Offer to interact with customers via toll-free phone and fax to provide as many points of potential contact with customers as possible.

Ensure that your sales and customer service staffers are fully conversant with e-mail and the web site functions, so they can quickly and seamlessly answer consumers' questions. Consumers usually don't mind answering a few questions about themselves that you can use to build a customer database. Meanwhile, gather relevant information about them that will make it easy for them to shop with you later.

You don't need a super-sophisticated product recommendation feature; even a place on your site where a customer can keep notes ("These three printers might work") or a self-reminder service (memo to self for Sept 30: order company holiday cards) will build a sense of partnership with customers.

Be sure to keep customers apprised as to the status of their orders. E-mail them to confirm receipt of the order, when it's shipped and the target arrival date, and to follow-up with a few post-sale questions. You'll endear yourself to all customers by including a personal touch—a handwritten note of thanks, free gift-wrap, a newsy note—with the order.

Finally, be sure that you've got the billing information correct. Provide as many opportunities for customers to post changes as practical and possible, and have employees spot-check the orders to ensure that customers truly understand what they're ordering.

## Keep the Conversation Going

As your relationship with your customers deepens, you'll want to find additional ways of letting them know about additional products and services that you've added. **Cross-selling** products to already happy, paying customers is a relatively easy, and usually highly profitable, way to increase your bottom line and market share at the same time.

Make sure that your sales reps, sales support staffers and customer service employees all know about your company's entire array of products and services—and why current customers might be interested in them. For instance, if one of your salespeople is concentrating on selling automated phone and voice-mail systems to medium-sized businesses, and another represents a line of headsets and high-tech wireless jacks that lets employees use their phones anywhere in the building, the two staffers need to swap leads and perhaps even conduct follow-up sales calls with each other's customers.

If reps resist, spend some time examining your sales incentive and bonus setup. Perhaps you've gained customers for years by having winner-take-all sales contests. But market conditions change, and if your customers are consolidating their preferred supplies from hundreds to just a few in each industry, it will benefit your whole company and your salespeople if you shift from a competitive to a cooperative sales compensation structure. You might form the sales staffers into teams that split the bonuses of all the lines they represent, or you might track customer retention and profitability, and phase in sales bonuses based on that, and not just on the basis of landing the big customer.

Many customers also like to hear stories about how other customers are using your products and services. When you've got a great war story from one customer—say, a machine shop was able to fill a lucrative rush order because of a new set of tools they'd purchased from you—ask that customer's permission to be featured in a customer newsletter or even in a press release. Not only does telling a real-life story get people's attention, but it also serves as an endorsement—after all, your solution worked for that customer, so you're likely to have good ideas for other customers, right?

Finally, make sure that the people who represent your company to the public are aware of how important it is to greet your customers warmly and to then efficiently handle their requests. Receptionists and administrative support staffers can set a positive tone for subsequent conversations and reinforce the entire company image that you are trying to project.

# Chapter 9

# Promotions and Advertising

Customers can't buy from you if they don't know you exist. Advertising and promotions literally put your company on the map by putting your logo and selling message in front of your buying public. Customers are more likely to buy from a company that they're familiar with. You can create familiarity through your ads, promotions, participation in trade shows, and other activities.

The exact mix of advertising and promotions that's right for your company depends on your distribution channels and how your products or services are sold. Ads and packaging are the non-human sales force that persuade consumers to choose your mass-marketed consumer product. Clerks in huge discount stores are few and poorly informed; if your target customer doesn't already have a good idea about the benefits of your product (as explained through advertising and promotions), that person will simply move on to another product that he or she does understand. On the other hand, salespeople for complicated, high-ticket items may rely on a general corporate image advertising campaign to set the tone for their extensive sales meetings with potential buyers.

## PLANNING MARKETING COMMUNICATIONS

Whatever you're selling, you'll need to communicate about it with your target buyers. Most businesses find that they need all three components of marketing communications (promotion, advertising and public relations, which is discussed in the next chapter), in some combination. Choosing the right balance of these three key components can be tough. Here's how:

**Step 1: Determine who is the target buyer** — Identification of exactly who is the target buyer, in demographic lifestyle, and other descriptive terms, is necessary before the construction of practical promotion, advertising and public relations (PR) programs.

**Step 2: Determine what is meaningfully unique about your product** — It's that unique positioning statement again. You need to define the features of your product or service that make it distinct from competitors in a way that will motivate customers to choose it over the competition.

**Step 3: Determine the best message to communicate your product positioning to target buyers** — The key to communicating product uniqueness and positioning is constructing a memorable unique positioning statement about product features and benefits that are meaningful to your target buyer. This may be a memorable slogan or ad message that correlates with the needs and wants of your target buyer. The ad message is a result of a carefully constructed positioning statement.

**Step 4: Determine promotion and advertising options, and costs in terms of available budget.** The possibilities are endless, but the money available is definitely finite. Small companies often find it practical to stress one of the three—promotion, advertising or PR—and relegate the other two to supporting roles.

A carefully crafted business positioning strategy can be used as a guideline for judging the appropriateness of all marketing programs, especially for promotion, advertising and PR events. It will ensure that your business image is consistent to your target buyers and help to build an enduring, memorable (and hopefully unique) message to sell your business products.

# Setting a Marketing Budget

Marketing support—which encompasses promotion, advertising, PR media relations, community relations, brochures, web sites and other materials—typically consumes 1 percent of net sales for industrial business-to-business operations to 10 percent (or more) for consumer packaged-goods companies. Retail stores usually spend 4 to 6 percent of net sales on marketing support. It's even more expensive when you're starting out. Consumer packaged-goods companies often figure that they'll spend about 50 percent of net sales of the new item on continuous marketing in the introductory year. That gradually subsides to 8 to 10 percent as consumers become familiar with the product.

It's all too easy to think that you'll pay for the cost-of-goods, overhead and salaries first and then think about what you might spend on marketing. Marketing can't survive on financial leftovers. After you've learned what the benchmark figures are for your industry and business model, budget at least that amount. Then, you can decide how to spend it among advertising, promotions and other marketing support vehicles.

### Work Smart

*Don't spend in a vacuum. Many trade groups routinely survey their members about promotional and advertising costs, and come up with industry averages. Knowing what the benchmarks are for your industry will help you create your own strategy, even if that strategy is to spend your budget in a dramatically different direction.*

*A word about the bucks: Schoenfeld & Associates of Lincolnwood, Illinois did a study outlining ad dollars as a percent of sales for various product categories. This may help to give you an idea of the "norm" in your field.*

### Advertising dollars as percentage of gross sales

| | |
|---|---|
| Grocery stores | 1.3 percent |
| Apparel | 2.9 percent |
| Soft drinks | 2.9 percent |
| Lawn/garden | 4.0 percent |
| Education | 5.0 percent |
| Computers | 5.1 percent |
| TV, radio, electronics | 5.3 percent |
| Catalog, mail order | 5.7 percent |
| Retail stores | 5.8 percent |
| Investment advice | 8.6 percent |
| Cosmetics | 10.4 percent |
| Confections | 10.6 percent |
| Memberships | 11.0 percent |
| Toys | 14.2 percent |
| Cleaning supplies | 14.5 percent |

When you're introducing yourself to the market, you'll no doubt have to spend more aggressively to establish your market share objective. You're trying both to win customers from competitors as well as to persuade customers that didn't know they needed or wanted your product that they do.

Once you're established, your goal is to maintain your market share and grow it steadily. Your percentage of total expenditures for promotion, advertising and PR should at least equal your market share, to maintain it.

You can't do every idea all the time. Here's a worksheet to help you size up the possibilities.

| Worksheet: PROMOTIONAL AND ADVERTISING BUDGETING | | | |
|---|---|---|---|
| *Promotions* | | | |
| **Type of Promotion** | **Cost** | **Frequency** | **Total Annual Cost** |
| *Samples* | | | |
| *Coupons* | | | |
| *Frequent-purchaser discounts or gifts* | | | |
| *Giveaways with purchase* | | | |
| *Giveaways without purchase* | | | |
| *Sponsorship* | | | |
| *Advertising* | | | |
| **Medium** | **Cost** | **Frequency** | **Total Campaign Cost** |
| *Television* | | | |
| *Newspaper—local* | | | |
| *Newspaper—metro* | | | |
| *Magazines* | | | |
| *Outdoor (billboards)* | | | |
| *Direct Mail* | | | |
| *Telemarketing* | | | |
| *Web site* | | | |
| *E-mail marketing* | | | |
| *Brochures* | | | |
| *Business Cards* | | | |
| *Trade Shows* | | | |
| **Event** | **Show Budget** | **Other Expenses** | **Total Show Cost** |
| | | | |
| | | | |

# PROMOTIONS

Most people associate promotions with giveaways—the ball bearing manufacturer that makes paperweights from heaps of bearings, the toys that fast-food companies use to bribe their youngest customers. In fact, promotions are better defined as direct *purchase incentives*— getting something for purchasing or nominating yourself as a sales prospect. Advertising, by way of contrast, outlines reasons to buy your product instead of the competition's.

Promotions can be fun. A creative campaign not only gets the attention of your potential customers, but also conveys a sense of your company's attitude and service. Most importantly, you can measure the results of a promotion to make sure that people actually are motivated to try out your product or service.

Typical promotional activities:

- games and contests

- premiums and gifts

- coupons and rebates

- product or service demonstrations

# Games and Contests

Have you ever left your business card in a bowl for a weekly drawing for a free lunch? Restaurants love such drawings not only because it doesn't cost them much to serve up a free lunch (still, the prize is a treat for the winner!), but because they get a fresh source of local businesses that might be interested in using the facility for meetings, events and dinners.

While you may not be able to afford a flashy contest, you can probably structure one that will help your target customers notice you. Start with a one-time experiment, asking not only for contact information but also a little about the potential customer's needs and business (a farm equipment distributor might inquire about the acreage the contestant manages, for instance).

Be sure to analyze the pool of entrants—if they're all already customers, or are somewhat poor prospects (if they all live far away), you're clearly not reaching the pool of potential customers you want. Your promotions must be designed to get people to buy from you; the market research you can conduct is just a secondary benefit.

Whatever games you devise, play fair with your customers. Don't charge them to enter, be sure to state how and when the winners will be selected, explain that the offer is void outside of a certain area and after a certain date, and remind players that any taxes are the responsibility of the winner. And be sure to check out the local laws with your attorney before you start any contest, game or drawing.

## Premiums and Gifts

This is the old "prize in the popcorn box" approach—a little something extra at no extra charge.

Premiums and gifts, sometimes called "ad specialties," are marketing staples. Who doesn't receive a calendar every December from a local realtor, auto maintenance mechanic or insurance broker? The modern version of this free gift idea is aimed at name awareness: magnets, calendars, luggage tags, T-shirts, pens, pencils or coffee mugs that carry your name, logo, and perhaps phone number or Internet address.

Anything that lasts and will be used by your prospective buyer can be effective. You may give these tokens out directly or have a buyer send in the proverbial "box top" and receive the valuable merchandise ...with your name all over it!

Find out what your competitors give away and come up with a fresh twist. Examine catalogs to see what logical fit you might find with your business; for instance, a candy company might produce its logo on a chocolate "computer" disc, or an online security firm might give away a padlock-shaped key chain.

The key question, as it is for any promotional activity, is whether the cost of the premiums or gifts will be recovered through increased business. If all your customers dutifully wear their T-shirts with your logo, will you gain new customers?

Monitoring results can be as easy as asking new customers how they heard about your business. If 99 percent tell you that they saw your ad in the Yellow Pages, you can be relatively confident that the premiums aren't doing what you hoped—if your goal was to attract customers. Premiums often are great reminders for current customers.

## Coupons and Rebates

Coupons good for a discount or a free sample are ubiquitous. There's a good reason why: Customers have to hand them over to get the benefit, and it's subsequently easy to track their effectiveness. Both existing and new customers appreciate a direct incentive to try, or re-try, your products or services. But customers also value their time; make the offer at least a 10 percent savings to attract their attention and make the bother of redeeming the coupon worth their while.

Only a small percentage of coupons are actually used. Newspaper coupon redemption rates in the grocery, drug and mass merchandise industry average between 1 percent and 5 percent. Redemption rates for other coupon delivery methods (e.g., mail, magazine, newspaper four-color inserts) vary widely, but still amount to less than 10 percent for most products.

Coupons attached to the product itself are the ones that are most likely to be used, with redemption rates of 20 to 50 percent. However, these coupons tend to be redeemed by existing customers, so if your intent in distributing coupons is to get new customers, find another way to get them to your targeted audience.

## Potential Pitfall

*Coupons come in many forms, but the one thing they* must *have in common is an expiration date! If you forget this, you'll live to regret it—you'll be redeeming those coupons forever. Don't forget to put on any other qualifying fine print, too, such as "one offer per household."*

A rebate is similar to a coupon, *except* that it is not honored at the time and point of purchase. Instead, the customer must complete and submit the rebate form, generally by mail. Only the most determined—and value-hungry—customers will go to the bother of redeeming a rebate. You'll also have to devote staff time to processing the rebates.

# Product Demonstrations

You can talk until you're blue in the face about your great product or service, but you'll win far more customers by showing rather than telling.

Demonstrations are an expensive, but extremely effective, way of reaching target customers. One recent study revealed that because of sampling, 51 percent of shoppers tried products they normally would not have tried, and 79 percent of those sampled bought the product when they felt they needed it.

The closer the demo is to the point of sale, the more likely potential customers are to translate their intrigue with the product or service into a decision to buy. It may be worth it to create a virtual demonstration of a process or unwieldy product, via video or CD.

Demos are effective because they give prospective customers a chance to see the product or service in action with their own eyes. Sales staffers get to explain what the prospects are experiencing or seeing. Demonstrations are particularly valuable as an effective (and often low-cost) way to introduce new products and new services. And because of the inherent drama, demos often spark a wave of word-of-mouth advertising.

## Work Smart

 *Demos come in many forms including open houses (to show off your new facilities), trade shows, local fairs, taste tests, test drives and seminars. Product demos are very effective, but service demos are sensational.*

*The popularity of seminars is growing, as they are effective in enabling service providers such as financial planners, physicians, and dealers in art and antique items to target and educate their potential customers.*

While you will generally want to reach your target audience when you conduct seminars, you can also use them to build your business's community image. For example, a good place to try out your seminar might be at a senior center. Every community has one, and they are often looking for program presenters. You don't want to put on a blatant commercial—just an informative, generic talk will win friends and influence people. The residents of the center may not be your top-priority target audience, but if you favorably impress them, others in the community will hear about it.

Especially when you're just starting out, it can be scary "giving away" your goods or services. What if people just take the freebies and waltz away without making a sale? This is especially worrisome for consultants, accountants and other professionals who are in knowledge industries. If information is what you're selling, why give it away?

Resist the temptation to give in to this fear. When you demo your product or service, you're showcasing your own credibility and mastery of the topic just as much as the actual product. When you confidently field questions tossed at you by an interested audience, you're showing people in a very convincing format how you'd work with them individually. When you promise to find out more and get back to someone who asks a question for which you don't have a complete answer, you're underscoring your honesty.

To be sure, choose your demo audience carefully. It's not a

coincidence that those yummy appetizer samples are usually given out in Saturday mornings in grocery stores—people shopping then are a little less likely to be rushing home from work to make dinner and have time to consider a new product. If you're starting out, you may not be able to get on the calendar of the most prestigious local executives' club right away. That's OK. Choose a group that may offer significant growth potential, such as a newly formed consortium of doctors who've just affiliated with a local hospital.

Service, technology and professional businesses can tap into dozens of venues that may serve up well-qualified audiences for their areas of expertise. As long as your talk is offering genuine help on its own, and isn't just a thinly veiled sales pitch, you're likely to be invited back. Consider:

- educational associations

- technical groups

- specialty trade groups

- clubs, sporting and hobby groups

- civic organizations

- groups that may be loosely gathered together by professional practices, such as hospital employees, lawyers' practices and accountants

- church members

- college groups, both of students and professors

- guest-teaching at local colleges as part of a course or seminar focused on your topic

- travel clubs, either independent or organized by local agents or travel clubs

# ADVERTISING

Advertising is impersonal, usually paid communication intended to inform, educate, persuade and remind.

Advertising is a sophisticated form of communication that must work with other marketing tools and business elements to be successful. Advertising must be interruptive—that is, it must make you stop thumbing through the newspaper or thinking about your day long enough to read or hear the ad. Advertising must also be credible, unique and memorable in order to work—and the target market must see the ads frequently enough to remember and act on them.

# Word-of-Mouth Advertising

Word-of-mouth advertising has existed as long as people have talked with each other. Personal endorsements and recommendations passed from one person to another are widely considered the most valuable sort of advertising—precisely because it appears spontaneous and unbiased.

In many respects, typical media advertising acts mainly as a catalyst to achieve word-of-mouth advertising and increased sales. Successful advertising will achieve many times more ad mentions through the word-of-mouth echo than the number of paid media presentations of the ads.

The question is, how can you touch off a round of word-of-mouth without appearing manipulative? You can try a direct approach by offering a discount or prizes to customers for leads and referrals that result in sales, but it's hard to come up with an incentive that will equally motivate each of your current satisfied customers.

Imaginative ads that resonate with the target audience, followed by a stellar sales, product, service and customer service experience, are the best ways to keep your word-of-mouth advertising on an upward spiral.

## Hints for Developing Effective Advertising

*Whether you work with an advertising agency or develop your ads yourself, you can use these criteria to help you create an attention-getting ad campaign.*

1.  ***Make sure your ads are "on strategy" with your business positioning.*** *A good positioning strategy ensures identification of the correct target audience for your advertising, along with a listing of meaningful features and benefits. It can provide reasons why the product is superior and unique and convey the personality of your company.*

2.  ***Communicate a simple, single message.*** *People have trouble remembering someone's name, let alone a complicated ad message. For print ads, the simpler the headline, the better. And every other ad element should support the headline message, whether that message is "price," "selection," "quality," or any other single concept.*

3.  ***Stick with a likable style.*** *Ads have personality and style. Find a likable style and personality, and stay with it for at least a year or more of ads. Changing ad styles and personality too often will confuse potential buyers. It also undermines the memorabilty of any one message.*

4. ***Be credible.*** *If you say your quality or value is the "best," and it is clearly not, word-of-mouth will speed your demise, not increase your business. Don't make yourself look bad by identifying and denigrating the competition. It is potentially confusing and distracting, and may backfire on you by making buyers more loyal to competitive products, not less.*

5. ***Ask for the sale.*** *Invite buyers to come to your store, send for more information, visit your web site, call for information or order directly through the ad. Provide easily visible information in the ad for potential customers to buy: location, telephone number, store hours, charge cards accepted and other relevant details.*

6. ***Make sure the ad is competitive.*** *Do your homework. Examine competitive ads in the media that you are planning to advertise in. Make sure your ad stands out from them—and at the same time doesn't have a style that's wildly inconsistent with your category. You can use personal judgment, a small focus group of target buyers (i.e., qualitative research), or more expensive sophisticated quantitative test methods. Compare ads for uniqueness, memorability, credibility and incentive to purchase.*

7. ***Make sure the ad looks professional.*** *If you have the time and talent, computer graphics and desktop publishing software can provide professional-looking templates to create good-looking print ads. Consider obtaining writing, artistic and graphics help from local agencies or art studios who have experienced professionals on staff, with expensive and creative computer software in-house. They may save you time and money in the long run, with better results. Electronic ads (e.g., TV, radio, Internet) and outdoor ads are best left to professionals to write, produce and buy for a fee or percentage of media dollars spent (i.e., generally 15 percent of gross media spending).*

8. ***Be truthful.*** *Whatever advertising medium you select, make sure your message is ethical and truthful. There are stringent laws regarding deceptive practices and false advertising.*

# Advertising Media

There's an old adage that holds that at least 50 percent of all advertising is a waste of money. It's probably true—and if you can figure out which half of your ad budget is useless, you'll save a bundle. But until you achieve this wisdom (which has so far eluded most marketers), you'd be wise to continue advertising full tilt and not take a chance on eliminating something that just might work.

Here's approximately how the average U.S. ad dollar is spent:

| Average U.S. Ad Dollar Spending Among Various Media | |
|---|---|
| *Type of Medium* | *Percentage* |
| Newspapers | 25 percent |
| Television | 25 percent |
| Direct Mail | 18 percent |
| Radio | 6 percent |
| Magazines | 5 percent |
| Billboards/Outdoor | 1 percent |
| Other | 20 percent |
| Total | 100 percent |

Most small businesses divide their advertising dollars among these categories:

- low- and no-cost advertising

- telephone directories and 800 numbers

- local print ads

- signs and displays

- higher-cost advertising alternatives

- direct mail and catalogs

- special advertising opportunities

- web sites and web advertising

## Low- and No-Cost Advertising

There are many things you can do in the way of advertising, promotion and publicity that cost little or nothing. And when you become successful enough to be able to afford more sophisticated ad techniques, you can officially test some of the more successful shoestring methods.

- Ask for **referrals**, consistently! Have ready a standard letter that you send to satisfied customers, with a self-addressed stamped envelope, requesting their brief endorsement and granting permission to quote them in sales literature.

- Choose a **simple logo** that quickly identifies your company.

- Print attractive and informative **business cards** that include your logo, and hand them out everywhere, consistently! If appropriate for your business, you can use your card as a discount certificate or other incentive. Or, you can have it placed on a magnetic backing so that it (hopefully) winds up on a refrigerator. If you use letterhead stationery in your business, have it match your business card. Keep your identity as consistent as possible.

- Print some **gift certificates**. These let your customers introduce you to new customers. Since you get paid up-front for the product or service, these are cash-flow friendly.

- **Birthday, holiday and seasonal cards** remind customers of the work you've done for them in the past.

- **Brochures** let you provide a lot of detail about your product or service. Simple three-fold brochure stock may be purchased from mail order suppliers such as Paper Direct (800-272-7377) in small quantities. This type of stock comes in attractive cuts and colors. Template software can be obtained that permits you to use your computer to generate classy looking brochures at minimal cost. Make your headline stand out. Cleverly use clip art or graphics. Give your customer as much quality information as you can pack into this identity piece. Keep it up-to-date and personalize it when possible (by writing in the margins or underlining specifics that might interest a particular prospective customer).

- If you have a slightly bigger budget, go for **slick four-color printed materials**. You'll need a printer who can do four-color separations, so if you're in a small town market with few hi-tech services, you may want to call a national firm that specializes in doing short runs. Firms such as MultiPrint (800-858-9999) do high-quality, low-cost work for small businesses. They also have a wealth of samples to get your creative ideas flowing.

- **Flyers** are the thrifty entrepreneur's dream. You can create them very inexpensively on your computer, or your local print shop can do them for you. You can use as much color as you like, with either a color printer or old-fashioned colored paper stock. Pack them full of information and post them on every bulletin board you can find that'll allow you space. Easy to distribute in bulk, these handy attention-getters can also be used as bag stuffers or inserts to put in with billings or to include when mailing payments to your suppliers. In fact, don't mail anything out of your business without including some little sales piece. Take advantage of piggybacking on that postage stamp. Placing stacks of flyers in building lobbies and tucking them under windshield wipers are done frequently, but you must be willing to alienate some people if you use these methods of distribution.

- **Doorhangers** are very effective and widely used by fast-food, home delivery and service businesses. If you choose this medium, don't scrimp on the quality of the paper stock. Make it heavy so it won't blow off doorknobs and litter the neighborhood. Add a coupon or some other incentive to your copy. Doorhangers are a good way to focus in on a specific target buyer.

- **Insert ads** are preprinted and then slipped into free shopper papers, as well as clutches of ads and fliers distributed by a centralized service. If you think that inserts could successfully reach your market, call one of the big distributors and learn how much it would cost you to try this kind of program. The industry leaders are ADVO (call 860-520-3200, and they'll give you the local contact) and Val-Pak, which is so big that you can look under "V" in most local phone books and find your neighborhood outlet. If you're just starting out, you may want to wait a bit before venturing into this zip code math contest, but keep it in mind as an opportunity for the future.

- If you could afford a billboard or a blimp, you probably wouldn't be reading this. But often you can create little **traveling billboards** at low cost. *Matchbooks* or *boxes* with a logo and vital information were always the thrifty solution, but nowadays smoking is on the wane. So try something different such as boxes with little toothpicks instead of matches. This has been very successful in several markets, particularly with upscale restaurants. *Key chains, pens* and *pencils,* and *calendars* are premiums and ad specialties. If they are appropriate for your kind of business, they're worth their weight in ad dollars. People use them. They don't usually end up in drawers or wastebaskets.

- *Bumper stickers, balloons, buttons, decals, and even T-shirts* are examples of **ad specialty signage** that works. Your local promotional supplier will have hundreds of examples of walking ads you can adapt to your needs.

- *Paper or plastic bags and packaging* make **economical billboards** too. Print your name, logo and message on anything you can, on all sides. Don't miss an opportunity to get your word out. Mailing labels are a perfect medium. Everyone who handles your mail will see your ad at no cost to you.

## Case Study — Mary Zentz, Real Estate Broker

*With a name like Mary Zentz, you'd think that this experienced residential real estate broker wouldn't have any trouble at all getting people to remember her.*

*Real estate is an exceptionally crowded field, though, and Zentz found when she started her business in the early 1990s that many great marketing ideas had already been claimed by competing brokers in her area. Eager to quickly gain market share, Zentz started a tireless three-year self-education effort. She read books on networking and on presenting herself gracefully in social and business situations, as well as how-to books aimed at homeowners and buyers—the better to understand the buyers and sellers she wanted to work with. She also joined a local business council and the local chapter of a national women business owners' association.*

*Simply joining those two organizations provided an inexpensive, but very effective advertising outlet: She started having her business card reprinted in their monthly member newsletters for only $25 each. Of course, the newsletters went to the relatively high-income groups of business owners and executives—a highly qualified self-selected audience. Next, Zentz contracted with a local freelance writer to produce a quarterly newsletter on home selling and buying written in the first person, as if Zentz herself had thought up every article.*

*But when it came to advertising, Zentz came up empty-handed. After a year of running a display ad in a well-read community newspaper, she was poorer by $3,500, but couldn't trace a single response from the ads (except for friends who saw the ads and hit her up for free garage sale signs).*

*Then Zentz got her bolt of inspiration. On a whim, she had a local caricature artist make up an exaggerated comic line drawing of her face at a local business fair. She liked it better than the professional photo of herself she'd been running in her newspaper ads, so she commissioned the caricature artist to come up with a whole year's worth of sketches, one for each month. She reprinted her business cards with the generic cartoon, and then redesigned the ads using the month-appropriate characters. Suddenly, the phone started ringing. She'd found a whimsical image that stuck in people's minds—and conveyed through the seasonally silly versions that she was a person who was fun as well as professional.*

When you're preparing direct mail pieces, don't go as cheaply as possible, figuring that 95 percent of them will end up in the trash anyway. You're still creating an impression with your pool of potential customers. Come up with an attention-getting black graphic and have it copied onto colored paper; formulate a provocative question or headline to draw people into the piece; and don't forget to provide a quick and easy way for customers to respond—through phone, mail or electronic format.

If you're targeting a relatively small, but affluent, group—such as lawyers, doctors, or other professionals or members of a select club or executive group—consider hand-addressing and hand-stamping the envelopes of a direct mail pitch or introductory piece. Hire someone (perhaps a teenager or retiree?) with graceful penmanship and give them plenty of time to complete the task. Hand-addressed envelopes receive much more personal attention and often get by administrative assistants, where as computer-labeled letters are often weeded out.

Look for clever, surprising ways to reach your target audience. One home-based cosmetics saleswoman realized that other moms were probably just as stressed as she with the whole Halloween rush. She made up 100 tiny sample makeup packets, inserted them with her business cards into envelopes addressed "to mom," and stapled them shut. She slipped them into the trick-or-treat bags of children who came to her door, and spent the next day setting up appointments with tired, grateful moms in her immediate neighborhood who were happy to spend a little time relaxing with a cosmetic-buying session.

Have a "Rolodex party" in which you and a friend in a complementary business. Get together in your office with your sales prospect Rolodexes, each find five of your own contacts who probably could use the services of your friend, and call them up on the spot to introduce each other.

Never underestimate the power of a "thank you." If someone's recommendation has netted you a huge sale, send them flowers or a restaurant gift certificate. Even if they've gone out of their way to put in a kind word for you, send a brief handwritten thank you.

Have some clever, seasonal and attention-getting oversized postcards printed up. You can add a seasonal or semi-personalized message on one side and a feature on the other, such as the schedule for the local high school's football season or spring landscaping clean-up tips.

Approach your local Service Corps of Retired Executives (SCORE) chapter and request a meeting with a retired advertising or marketing director. Show mock-ups of your advertising and promotional plans, in as much detail as possible, to the SCORE rep and ask him to recommend changes. You may want to schedule several sessions so you can fine-tune your prototypes with him before spending the money to produce the material. (SCORE is a free service provided by the federal Small Business Administration; check www.score.org for a listing of SCORE contacts in your area.)

*Frequency* and *consistency* are key to effective advertising. Always send the same message, and send it whenever the opportunity arises.

## It Worked for Them!

*Kimberly Stansell had some big ideas about translating her hobby of making jewelry into a mail-order business. She had the design and metalworking elements down cold, but had no idea how to even start designing a catalog, never mind frame and launch a mail-order firm.*

*She approached SCORE, which linked her with a retired head of catalog operations for Sears, Roebuck. He gave her hours of priceless insight, for free. Los Angeles-based Stansell subsequently became so good at promoting her jewelry that she launched a small business marketing newsletter called the "Bootstrappin' Entrepreneur."*

## Generating Word-of-Mouth Online

Online services can seem like the perfect venue for generating a wave of word-of mouth advertising about your product.

And it can be—to a point. While the Internet is no longer the exclusive purview of scientists who freely flame hapless commercial souls, there are still many unwritten rules about tooting your own horn in cyberspace. Here are some tips:

- Choose the venues where you'd like to spread the word about your company as carefully as you'd choose any other medium. Explore the chat room, listserv or bulletin board thoroughly, over a period of several weeks, to see how respectfully others treat each other, if moderators ban commercial endorsements, and what seems to happen when a specific product or service is plugged by a respected member.

- Establish yourself as a trusted participant before recommending yourself. Make informed, short, to-the-point commentaries that genuinely help others. Even in the process of doing that, you'll look like a pro to the other participants, and you may start to receive inquiries through private e-mails that can be turned into sales leads.

- Query the chat group, listserv, or bulletin board leader to see if you might serve as an expert host on a topic on which you're qualified.

- If you do recommend your own product or service, don't be coy. State up-front what your relationship to the product or service is. At the same time, don't forget to direct people to your own web site.

- If you're in doubt, ask the advice of a seasoned surfer who also hangs around the venue.

- Don't overstay your welcome. Shrug off barbs from other Internet users who may not sympathize with your aspirations for your business, but don't insist on pushing your product in every exchange.

## Telephone Directories and Toll-Free Numbers

Advertising in telephone directories is, for some businesses, critically important. But it's definitely not cheap! Publishers of these directories have stringent guidelines that make it hard for you to distinguish your ad from your competitors' without spending a lot of money. If you go with this kind of ad, check out the alternatives—Sprint, MCI, Ameritech, Southern Bell, whatever baby Bell you have in your area, as well as the cellular firms such as AT&T and Cellular One. Many areas receive directories published by more than one company. The cost of advertising varies, as does the market served. Try to pick the one that best targets your potential customers at the lowest cost.

Get all their prices and pick their reps' brains for information and advice. (But don't confuse a sales pitch for advice.) Be very careful making your listing category choice. Do you want to position yourself as "pizza" or "restaurant" or "carry-out?"

Even if you have to stretch to afford it, go for the bold-type listing if you can afford only a single line listing. If you can manage it, a display ad will probably pay big dividends if you keep it running year after year. Use strong black borders and get the most size for the money without sacrificing placement. Don't be afraid to use lots of copy and use pictures and color (red is the usual alternative) if your budget can handle it.

Try to give your business a solid, dependable, reliable feel in your ad. If appropriate, say that you're insured or mention that you've been in business a long time. List every service you can think of, as well as your hours, and put some stress on your location so people can relate to it. Ask to see prototypes of successful ads in your industry.

**Toll-free numbers.** The cost of your own toll-free phone number may be less than you may think. Competition has made this a bargain for buyers to reach you, though packages and prices are constantly changing. When you're comparison shopping among phone companies, don't forget to ask about upgrades and options, such as call-forwarding to any line you choose. Of course, if you do spring for a toll-free number, you'll want to splash it over all your new-customer advertising and promotional material—and include your non-toll-free office number for routine calls.

# Local Print Ads

Classified ads and small display ads in local newspapers or magazines are a good way to reach your buyers. Get **media kits** from all your local publications (and any regional or national publications you may want to use as a model). Take a look at what they have to offer and at what price. The media kit will give you the demographic and geographic reach of the publication as well as how much the publisher charges for different types and frequencies of ads.

Remember that the lowly classifieds are perused by a huge number of people, especially on weekends. Big-time auto dealers and real estate agents fill up these pages for a reason. If you slip a classified ad into the right category and keep it running consistently, you'll probably get a response strong enough to at least pay the cost of the ad.

The same rules apply to small display ads as to classifieds. Make it easy for your prospective buyers to learn what you have to offer. Use a border to set your ad apart. Run the ad in the appropriate publication—do your homework, read those media kits. Make it very easy for your buyer to respond to your offer by giving a clear phone number, address and location details if space permits.

# Sample Advertisements

*InHouse is a San Francisco retail store that specializes in home office design and furnishings. Its mission is to help professionals with home offices create functional, ergonomically correct work environments that aren't stylistically or aesthetically jarring with the rest of the home.*

YOU NEED TO

TURN THAT

CLOSET INTO A

HOME OFFICE

THAT WORKS?

NO PROBLEM. COME TO
**InHouse**
THE HOME OFFICE FURNITURE SPECIALISTS

DESKS ■ CHAIRS ■ LAMPS ■ ACCESSORIES
ASK ABOUT OUR SALE ITEMS
343 Vermont Street, between 16th & 17th Streets
San Francisco, California  Open Tuesday - Saturday, 10 - 6

Phone 415.554.1950

*Owner and designer Mark Dutka wanted to communicate through the print ads that he and his staff have the expertise and products available to help homeowners with awkward spaces, multiple-demand work spaces, and other home-office idiosyncracies. The ads are intended to motivate home-office workers to look critically at their current spaces with an eye towards upgrading through InHouse. The print ads run in San Francisco, an upscale regional magazine, and the San Francisco Chronicle, a major metropolitan daily newspaper.*

YOU WORK AT HOME
AND YOU'RE TIRED OF SITTING
AT THE KITCHEN TABLE?

NO PROBLEM. COME TO
**InHouse**
THE HOME OFFICE FURNITURE SPECIALISTS

DESKS ■ CHAIRS ■ LAMPS ■ ACCESSORIES
ASK ABOUT OUR SALE ITEMS
343 Vermont Street, between 16th & 17th Streets
San Francisco, California  Open Tuesday - Saturday, 10 - 6

Phone 415.554.1950

*The InHouse staff has a checklist that enables them to keep track of where shoppers first heard about the store. Simultaneously, Dutka's media relations firm has successfully positioned him as an expert on ergonomic design for home offices; consequently, he has appeared in multiple local and regional articles on workspace design.*

With an annual advertising budget of only $50,000, Gayle Fisher is expected to let the world know of the charms of north central Montana. As executive director of the Russell Country Tourism Bureau, Fisher's goal is to build awareness of the area, which is best known for its dinosaur fossil excavation fields, cowboy heritage, and connections with the Oregon Trail and Lewis and Clark expedition.

She allots about $4,000 for creation of the 1/6th size print ads and the remainder for buying the space to run them in magazines such as Montana magazine, Better Homes and Gardens, and Midwest Living. Would-be tourists respond to the ad via the toll-free number, which connects them to Montana's centralized tourism information hotline; the state also sends out brochures and booklets about attractions in Montana.

# DIG THESE BONES.

Some people think digging up dinosaur bones is a real kick. Other folks prefer finding bones assembled in a museum. In Russell Country, we cater to both. For our free travel planner, call

**800-527-5348.**

RUSSELL COUNTRY MONTANA

http://travel.mt.gov/Russell/

# "LOOK CLARK, A HOTEL WITH CABLE."

Russell Country is a lot more civilized than it used to be. And with plenty of historic attractions, including the new Lewis & Clark Interpretive Center, it's a lot more fun. For our free travel planner, call

**800-527-5348.**

RUSSELL COUNTRY MONTANA

http://travel.mt.gov/Russell/

MONTANA'S MOUNTAIN TRAIL

GET LOST. TAKE A HIKE. HIT THE TRAIL.

Many rewards await those who explore the unspoiled terrain of Montana's Mountain Trail. If you enjoy secret hikes and scenic heights, Russell Country is the place to lose your worries and find nature's most unique pleasures. For our free travel planner, call

1-800-527-5348.

RUSSELL COUNTRY

Box 3166
Great Falls, MT 59403
http://travel.mt.gov/Russell/ MONTANA

MONTANA'S HERITAGE TRAIL

TALL TALES & TIMELESS TRAILS.

From the proud ancestry of our Native American forefathers to the adventurous spirit of Charlie Russell and Lewis & Clark, our land is rich with heritage. Celebrate Russell Country's history by visiting the monuments and museums dedicated to the legends who made the West. For our free travel planner, call 1-800-527-5348.

RUSSELL COUNTRY

Box 3166 • Great Falls, MT 59403
http://travel.mt.gov/Russell/ MONTANA

Fisher changes the theme of the ads every three years or so to keep interest in the region fresh. In 1999, she adopted a humorous set of ads (above) emphasizing benefits to tourists such as the wide variety of activities to choose from. This campaign replaced a more straightforward approach (left) that listed the types of sites in the region.

## Signs and Displays

Flag your location to the world through a sign that captures the essence of your company.

Billboards, blimps, searchlights and skywriting are exotic and expensive, so you'd be better served by concentrating on more down-to-earth signs. Start with your vehicles. Cars and trucks are great traveling billboards. You can readily find a magnetic sign supplier who can fashion a flexible rubberized sign to attach to your company truck or your personal car. When not in use for company business, simply remove the sign.

Interior and exterior signs should be lighted to take advantage of every opportunity to be seen. Within the parameters allowed by local zoning ordinances, work with a local sign shop to come up with a consistent look for all your signs.

## Potential Pitfall

*When you create posters and banners, be aware that using all capital letters sometimes hampers readability and be sure to check scrupulously for spelling errors.*

**Point-of-purchase displays.** No matter how much advertising and promotion you do, a retail customer still has to make that final decision to choose your product over your competitor's. Point-of-purchase (POP) displays can nudge them in your direction. Often, manufacturers pay the cost of POP advertising for retailers that carry their lines. Careful collaboration with the retailers can result in display that enhances their stores, conveys your company's image, and moves product.

POP can take the form of danglers, signs, posters, banners, custom display racks, special lighting or video monitors with promotional loops playing all day long. Bounceback and register tape coupons (printed on the back of the cash register receipt) are good to give at a POP location to stimulate customer's return to your business in the future. POP even has its own trade magazine, *POP Times*, 7400 Skokie Blvd., Skokie, IL 60077 (847-675-7400). If you are a retailer or a maker of consumer goods, you'll want to study the opportunities POP offers.

## Higher-Cost Advertising Alternatives

Once you've bootstrapped yourself into fast growth, you will probably want to start working with a local marketing consultant who can help you set strategy and work with advertising and public relations agencies.

Ad agencies typically collect a 15 percent commission on the media buys—that is, what they pay on your behalf to reserve space in a print medium or time in a broadcast medium. As well, you'll have to allow thousands, possibly tens of thousands of dollars, for developing the creative message that actually is printed or broadcast.

Here's a rundown of the major alternatives:

- Metropolitan newspapers reach hundreds of thousands of readers, especially in the Sunday editions. Ask about zoned sections that might target just your county or cluster of suburbs, or a portion of the city.

- Local and regional magazines are often surprisingly affordable, especially for smaller-sized display ads. Ask about special themed issues on topics such as computers, health and various consumer topics, such as weddings, for very targeted advertising opportunities.

- National magazines sometimes offer special zoned advertising sections, but even these are very expensive.

- Local and cable television time is typically sold in 30- and 60-second time slots. Sometimes you can get a good deal by arranging to have your ad fill in the schedule, which means you'll get a mix of prime-, shoulder- (medium-) and low-demand time.

- Radio is often useful for reaching very specific demographics, not the least of which is the car-bound commuter during morning and evening rush hours.

- Billboards and other outdoor advertising vary widely in cost, depending on location and size.

## Work Smart

*The proliferation of cable channels has moved local market television advertising within reach of many small businesses. Creating a smooth television ad is more complicated than just turning your home video camera on your office and employees.*

*A broadcast radio or television ad requires:*

- *a producer to help you set the overall budget and plan*

- *a scriptwriter to crystallize your message and company image into words, sound effects and images*

- *a graphic designer to create labels, maps and words, and to create an overall look for the ad*

- *a special effects guru, if you want animation or other glitzy effects*

- *at least one voice-over artist to narrate or conduct the conversation*

- *a camera crew to film a television ad*

- *a studio crew to produce a radio ad*

- *a production crew in an any case, to blend together the elements*

- *a media buyer to help you evaluate which stations and time slots will best reach your intended audience, and to then purchase the time slots during which your ad will appear (for a 15 percent or more commission)*

*One low-cost option is to purchase rights for your market to an already-successful ad produced by a large company in your category in another market. AdvantEdge Television Advertising, Inc., (AdedgeTv@aol.com) does just that.*

## Telephone and Internet Marketing

Telemarketing comes in various guises. We all gripe about the computer-dialed boiler room selling operations that pester us at dinnertime, but there are other ways of using the phone as a sales tool.

You'll probably be most comfortable calling people you've been referred to by current clients or networking contacts. Consider telephone contact as a way of giving out information or keeping in touch, and avoid thinking of it as a way to close a sale. Calling on former customers to thank them for their business and inform them of new products or ideas is a good way to keep in touch with a pre-qualified client base. If you're a determined person convinced that telemarketing is the best choice for your business, take a look at a book called *Successful Telephone Selling in the '90s*, by Martin D. Shafiroff and Robert L. Shook, published by Harper Collins.

The marketing mores of cyberspace are still evolving. While spamming, or posting hundreds of identical marketing messages via free bulletin boards, newsgroups and chat groups, is still considered bad form, widely accepted forms of online marketing are emerging. Ways to gain a voice online include:

- Maintain a constantly fresh web site. Change the date on your site daily, update your content, and periodically ask colleagues to spin through the site to be sure it's easy to navigate and doesn't contain any dead links.

- Request reciprocal links with sites with which you have an affinity, such as suppliers' and vendors' sites.

- Target banner advertising on sites frequented by your target customers. A sporting goods store might want to advertise on the segment of a local calendar that includes when local sports teams play.

- Cooperate with sites that provide a forum for local advertising. These might be under the auspices of the Chamber of Commerce, local newspaper, or a private or government-sponsored business development group.

- Participate in small-business cooperatives offered by mega-sites such as Amazon.com. You can get a toehold into e-commerce by offering products related to your business via an e-commerce vendor that helps you customize part of your site to sell its products.

- Provide minimally intrusive direct-marketing options, such as an e-mail newsletter or monthly sales fliers.

- Be sure to respect the privacy of people on your e-mail list and those who register at your web site. Clearly post your privacy policy.

To keep up with the rapidly changing Internet marketing world., subscribe to the free newsletter offered by interactive advertising agency Doubleclick, at www.doubleclick.com.

## Formulating an Effective Web Site

Coming up with a web site that is easily used and understood by anyone who might happen by is harder than it looks. Even though you don't know who those people might be, you need to read their minds by making it immediately obvious how to use and move around your site. Chances are you'll end up hiring a specialist to at least develop the graphics and do the programming for your web site. Still, you're in charge of the information on it and how well it serves your current and potential customers.

First, decide what the purpose of your site will be. Will it only inform, or will you integrate e-commerce and e-customer service into it? Formulate a rough flow chart of how you would like to guide visitors through the site.

Every site, no matter how big or small, must include these elements:

- Full company identification, including real-world address. Potential customers, especially, may want reassurance that you "really exist," especially if much of your communication with customers occurs electronically.

- Multiple ways to contact you, through pop-up email screens, phone, fax and snail mail.

- An "About" section that briefly explains what your company is and what it does.

- A "Who We Are" section that provides an overview of key company officers and their responsibilities, including direct-contact e-mail addresses.

- A "What We Do" section that explains what your company does and how it helps its customers. Customer referrals, stories and summaries of successfully completed projects may branch out from here.

If your site exists only to stake out a millimeter of cyberspace for your company, you can still make sure it's genuinely informative. To be sure, use preexisting written material as a jumping off point, but it's counter-productive to simply shovel brochures onto the Internet. You'll want to reshape the material and take advantage of the infinite flexibility of the electronic medium to go much more in-depth than you ever could in mere print.

For instance, if you have a paragraph in your brochure stating that your company has been owned and operated by the same family since 1933, you might want to make a short, amusing family history on the web site that tells how your great-great grandpa came up with the original business concept. It could be an internal link from the "Who We Are" section.

Aim for a bright, lively look and feel. Use large type and easy-to-read colors. You might include a Frequently Asked Questions section to make first-time site visitors feel at home.

Beef up your informational site with case histories that provide an inside glimpse into how your product or service directly benefits your customers. (Of course, get the customers' permission first—you may have to leave their identity out altogether.) Show how your industry is growing and explain what your plans are to grow with it. List credentials of key company players.

Do remember, though, that cyberspace is just as public as any other place. Don't post information that you wouldn't feel comfortable being printed in your community newspaper. Hints about new products, very optimistic and specific sales and profit projections, and too much personal information about company principles are out of place.

# Worksheet: WEB SITE PLANNING

*Who is the intended audience for the web site?* _____
_____
_____

*What department or individual will be responsible for the site?* _____
_____
_____

*What departments will contribute part of their budgets to the site's development and maintenance?* _____
_____
_____

*How will the site be regularly updated and maintained? Who will be responsible for that?* ____
_____
_____

*Will the site include e-commerce capabilities? If so, how will the following corporate functions be integrated into the site?*

- *Accounts receiveable/payment processing* _____
_____

- *Order processing* _____
_____

- *Communicating status of orders to customers* _____
_____

- *Fielding customer inquiries* _____
_____

- *Integrating order fulfillment and inventory management electronically* _____
_____

- *Tracking order fulfillment in-house* _____
_____

- *Tracking status of shipments* _____
_____

- *Handling returns and complaints* _____
_____

*How will you integrate existing logos and graphic design elements into the site to keep a consistent corporate style?* _____
_____
_____

_____

*How will you promote the site through traditional media, search engines and otherwise?* _____

_____

_____

*How will you evaluate the success and return on investment of the site?* _____

_____

_____

Blending e-commerce into your site? That's a whole new ball of wax.

Soliciting customer orders over the Internet is far more complicated than just printing out some e-mails, trotting them over to inventory, filling and shipping them. Unless you anticipate an extremely low volume of orders to be sent electronically, you will likely have to integrate the e-commerce orders into your overall flow of processing and fulfilling orders. That might mean upgrading and changing your entire computer network and many related order-processing and customer-support functions. As well, if your fulfillment, warehousing and shipping operations are behind the times—say, if you aren't using bar codes and hand-held computer scanners for inventory control—you may be forced to upgrade those functions, as well.

Additional training on the new integrated and e-commerce system will help employees become familiar with the technology, the rules of proper etiquette when responding to customer e-mails, and other operational issues. If you skimp on the "invisible" operations, your web site could gum up the smooth-running operations that you've worked hard on. And as life would have it, the crunch retail seasons will put even more pressure on you to be sure that you can fill the orders pouring in, as people become very worried that the gifts they ordered will arrive at the right houses on the right dates.

Designing an e-commerce site can be tricky. Even coming up with universally understood keywords for the internal search engine can be nerve-wracking, as you try to anticipate exactly how each of thousands (hopefully) of web visitors will ask the same question as they try to find what they want. You'll need to break down merchandise into logical categories, then decide how much content to weave into the site, where you'll get that content, and how closely aligned the content will be with the actual products and services you sell. So far, successful sites have developed a model of offering content as a subsection of the site—a magazine within the site, if you will—while embedding a few internal hyperlinks into the body of the content that whisk site visitors to the page where they can order the item they were just reading about.

Customer feedback and comment is a vital part of any successful web site. Offer customers not only the e-mail addresses of several company contacts, but also phone and fax numbers so they can reach customer service representatives to solve problems. The closer your customer support via phone is to the 24-hour Internet availability, the more customers will take your site seriously.

Of course, you'll have to have an entire electronic checkout process; order verification via-email; constant e-mail updates and reminders of the status of the order; and a clearly defined, prominently positioned privacy policy. And while you're sorting out all these issues, you'll also have to be figuring out how you'll tell people about your site—an effort that may require traditional advertising.

The great thing about e-commerce is that it is always available and always on. Customers can get basic questions about your company answered even while you're out playing golf; customers can help themselves to your virtual shop while you're in Mexico. In order to reinforce that message of "we never close," be sure that the customer service phones are always manned, even if that means forwarding calls to your home office during the weekend.

## Direct Mail and Catalogs

Direct mail and catalogs are mainstays for time-pressed households and are gaining enormous popularity. Most categories are dominated by very large national companies with formidable market presence and resources. If you even hope to get started in this arena, start very small and narrow your niche to a needlepoint.

Whether you use direct mail promotions or develop your own catalog, the demographics of your mailing list, or database, is the key to success. Choosing, buying, maintaining and using a mailing list is a sophisticated database application process that is best undertaken with the counsel of a list management firm or consultant.

Customers are unforgiving when it comes to promptness, recordkeeping and customer service. They'll expect a toll-free 24-hour ordering line, every detail of every catalog item at the tip of the sales clerk's tongue, and near-immediate delivery. That means that you'll have to organize and manage a top-notch warehouse of inventory, staffed with sharp, motivated, detail-oriented fulfillment and shipping clerks—or an expensive computerized equivalent.

With this daunting list of logistics, you may want to start by farming out the order-taking to a commercial call center and focusing mainly on marketing and fulfillment.

## Specialized Advertising

Trade shows are essential to many types of wholesale and manufacturing businesses. At a trade show, suppliers of all sorts to a particular industry or on a particular theme set up shop temporarily in booths in a convention or show center. Usually workshops and seminars on industry trends and how-tos are held simultaneously in the same center. (Consumer trade shows—which have themes such as garden or baby shows, are held in a trade show format in a local convention center, and are open to the public—are really a form of community event and are addressed in that portion of Chapter 10.)

Participating in trade shows can be very expensive, but it also may be essential to win the attention and respect of influential retail buyers. They're also prime trawling grounds for serious networking; not only will you be talking to potential customers, but you can also seek out other companies with complementary products and services with whom you might develop joint marketing programs or products. You'll also gain lots of insight from the educational sessions. Because there's so much to do at a trade show, plan to bring at least a couple of employees so you can get as much out of the event as possible.

Trade shows themselves are a profitable business, which explains why there are so many to choose from. You may be faced with some tough decisions about which ones to attend—the big, expensive national show that's the single annual must-go, or the less popular, but more affordable, regional show where you're less likely to be lost in the shuffle? Weigh not only the price and convenience of going, but also the quality and number of prospective customers you're likely to encounter. Only since the late 1990s has the attendance of trade shows been audited with any level of credibility. Quiz the show promotors about exactly who attends their show and for how long. Press for proof from a certified independent auditing firm; if a show isn't audited, that's a sign that its claims about the number and quality of attendees has probably been exaggerated over the years.

Participating in a show involves quite a bit more than just showing up. Here's a countdown of items to help you leverage your presence at a show most effectively:

- See if you have any area of expertise that can be showcased in a workshop, panel discussion, speech or seminar. Check with the show organizers at least four months in advance to see what mix of speakers and topics they are trying to get for the show. Be sure to position yourself not just as the owner of a company, but as an expert in an industry topic in your own right. If you score a speaking gig, prepare letters and postcards to promote your soapbox moment to probable show-goers several times before the show starts. You'll gain status even in the eyes of those who can't make it to hear your presentation.

- Find out the mix of attendees to the show and determine which ones represent your best prospects. Review your sales material to see if you need to add or adapt any to specifically address the concerns of the buyers you're likely to find at the show.

- If you've never participated in a show before, you'll have your hands full preparing a booth and exhibit. The great strength of trade shows is that it's a show—a place where you're expected to show what your product or service can do. Think of ways you can actively—live, on video tape or through computer animation—demonstrate not just what your product or service does, but directly how it benefits your target market, as represented at the show. For instance, if you've concocted a miracle cleaning solvent that cuts in half the time it takes to disinfect floors, you might stage a demo floor-cleaning contest at a show for janitorial firms, but you might also have a computer-animated graphic illustrating the time and cost saving engendered by use of the product for a show that targets health care industry executives. People love show-and-tell. Capitalize on that and the novelty factor by coming up with clever, truthful ways to dramatize your product or service.

- Work with a local exhibit design firm to translate your corporate logo and graphic look into a booth with effective signs, backdrop, lighting, and enough table and display space. Don't forget to include seating for your company reps as well as storage space for materials and samples.

- Estimate the cost of participating in the show by looking into the expense of building, shipping, setting up and taking down your exhibit. Be aware that union rules at many convention centers can considerably add to the cost and frustration of setting up, in particular. Also factor in the cost of any materials and samples you give away; travel, hotel and meal cost for yourself and employees; and hospitality expenses for taking out prospective and current customers.

- Prepare a pre-show advertising mini-blitz. Postcards inviting prospects to visit you (list your booth number and location) and personalized e-mails are effective. Make appointments to see hot prospects, but also leave time in your show schedule to prowl the aisles, scoping out the competition.

- Come up with a way to track who drops by the booth and how to collect their names and contact information, so that you can later qualify and follow-up on your prospects.

- Train employees—and yourself, if necessary—in the fine art of trade show hospitality. Gum-snapping employees occupied by flirting with the cute attendee across the aisle aren't going to help you promote your company. Review introductory patter, sales pitches, and follow-up techniques with everyone who will attend. Instruct employees who aren't going how they'll be involved with follow-up.

- Many shows attract a surprisingly large contingent of international buyers. Think through your response should a representative of an overseas company approach you about becoming a sales rep for you, or request information about availability of your products and services in his country. If this is a possibility and language might be a barrier, line up translation services that you can call in a temporary basis if needed. Consider having a small portion of sales material professionally translated into the languages that you think are most likely to be requested.

- Use downtime during the show to start following up with prospects you've already connected with. Have the home office start assembling packets to send out and line up follow-up sales appointments for you.

**Co-op advertising** with another business, a national association, or suppliers can help you get big-budget advertising for a local charge.

The parameters of your co-op advertising opportunities may be spelled out quite specifically by a franchise or business license agreement under which you operate. If that's so, you may be able to reap some impressive economies of scale with other franchisees in your region to pool some of your advertising money to buy big display ads in local newspapers that list all of your locations. As well, carefully examine your agreement before launching a clever campaign on your own. You may discover that the franchiser has the right to approve and modify any ad you run. Your agreement may also restrict certain types of ads or certain types of publications or other ad outlets. You'll also want to find out what is booked on the national organization's ad schedule so that you don't end up duplicating or contradicting one of their campaigns.

In any case, be sure to pump your marketing contact at your association or supplier for tips on how to get the most from buying, placing and following up on the ad that you jointly sponsor with them. Just because you're getting a slick ad and some money to run it locally doesn't mean that you won't have to make some key decisions about what publications or broadcast outlets to run it in and how your co-op partner may want you to follow-up. Find out what techniques have worked well for localities similar to yours and adapt their successes to your own situation.

## It Worked for Them!

*What if you haven't got a national supplier or franchiser with a set of ready-made ads you can co-opt for co-ops? Create your own!*

*When two national chains of educational toy stores started pushing into their metropolitan market, small neighborhood toy stores who'd been around for decades started to get worried. They'd gotten to know each other through industry groups and had occasionally discussed the possibility of joining forces to buy large, co-sponsored ads in big metropolitan newspapers, rather than dividing their efforts among myriad community papers, with less impact. But, even though they were widely dispersed throughout the area, they'd somehow had the vague sense that they'd be competing with each other if they linked up in a major ad effort.*

*Nothing unites like a common enemy. As soon as news of the imminent invasion of the big chains leaked out, the storeowners were on the phone lining up a meeting to suddenly get their co-op idea rolling.*

*The 20 stores officially formed a regional alliance, which not only gave them a group alliance, but also gave them a legal entity that could collect the co-op money, create the ads and buy the space. They came up with a slogan—"All toys teach. Do you like what your children are learning?"—that they agreed to put in all ads they ran. They set up a toll-free phone number that customers could use to get directions to the nearest store, and that the store owners themselves could use to scout up items that they didn't have on hand, but that another member store might have. That way, customers had access to inventory at all the stores when they shopped at just one.*

*They also shared ideas that worked, such as collaborating with local schools to stock books, as well as science and craft kits that coordinate with their curriculum, and supporting the schools' fund-raising events.*

*The result? Each of the stores saw a year-over-year increase in sales—despite the fact that the chains made splashy debuts.*

## Worksheet: PROMOTION PLANNING

*What target audience are you trying to attract with the promotion?* _____
_____
_____

*How will you qualify participants (by returning a direct-response postcard: by demographic, age or other criteria)?* _____
_____
_____

*If the promotion has clear winners and losers, how will you reward winners?* _____
_____
_____

*How will you publicize the promotion and its winner?* _____
_____
_____

*What actions will prevent losers from feeling angry and let down (consolation prizes, thanks for being good sports, coupons for a nominal giveaway at your business or other measures)?* _____
_____
_____

*If the promotion is designed to elicit qualified leads for later follow-up, exactly how will you follow-up?* _____
_____
_____

*What is the cost of the promotion?* _____
_____
_____

*How will you measure the direct impact on sales and profits (return on investment)?* _____
_____
_____

*If the promotion involves custom-produced items, what will you do with leftovers?* _____
_____
_____

## Worksheet: ADVERTISING PLANNING

*What target audience are you trying to attract with the advertising?* _____
_____
_____

*How does this medium reach people in that audience (determine this by examining media kits)?* _
_____
_____

*How many times must you advertise before you can reasonably expect people to recognize and respond to your ad?* _____
_____
_____

*How much does this medium cost? Can you get any add-ons included in the cost of the basic ad (such as, getting one print color added if you buy 10 or more ads in a six-month span)?* _____
_____
_____

*What other media reinforce this medium, and how should you allot your advertising dollars among them for maximum impact (short radio ads often cite snappy web site addresses, for instance)?* _
_____
_____

*How will you measure the direct impact on sales and profits (return on investment)?* _____
_____
_____

# Chapter 10

# Media, Community and Professional Relations

Public relations may be the single most misunderstood element of an overall marketing plan. It's not, as many hope, simply "free publicity" for your company. It is the art of working with media with the aim of creating a broad and deep awareness of your company's areas of expertise, and how your products and services benefit your customers. Professional and community relations are much more straightforward, as anyone who has ever worked on an industry committee or has been asked to contribute to the latest downtown flower-planting effort can attest.

As we discussed in Chapter 9, word-of-mouth advertising is widely considered to be the single most effective way of establishing a credible company reputation and drawing in customers. An assertive public relations campaign is the ultimate word-of-mouth leverage—utilizing the mouth of one person—a reporter—to spread the word to thousands.

When you advertise, you're in charge of the content and look of the ad, as well as where it runs. Not so with public relations. *Your goals will be accomplished only by cultivating mutually trusting relationships with editors and writers who speak to your target market.* You're not paying for the media exposure, so you won't have much control over when and how your comments are used. The key to a successful media relations campaign is to understand the reporting process—along with a healthy dose of patience.

# CHOOSING TARGET MEDIA

The media with whom you want to develop the most mutually beneficial relationships are those that have direct, regular influence with your customers and end users. It might seem glamorous to be profiled in glowing terms on a prime-time network news magazine, but national exposure actually might do less for you than you might fantasize. Business-to-business marketers, especially, as well as companies with limited geographical markets, might get absolutely nothing from such coverage—until it was picked up as a news item in a trade magazine or community newspaper.

Media outlets (most of which have corresponding web sites) that have direct, regular credibility with your target market may include:

- **Trade magazines** — These cover industry issues in great depth. Editors are usually very well versed in the industry. These magazines have relatively small, but very tightly targeted, circulations and usually aren't sold on newsstands.

- **General interest business magazines and newspapers** — *The Wall Street Journal, Crain's New York Business, Crain's Chicago Business, Business Week, Forbes, Fortune, The Economist* and others cover topics of interest to most business people, such as legislation, societal and market trends, and matters of the national and global economy. They're widely available on newsstands.

- **Special interest business magazines** — These zero-in on niches that have wide appeal to the public at large. *Inc., Fast Company, Home Office Computing* and *The Industry Standard*, for instance, are all sold on newsstands, but mainly attract readers interested in small businesses, fast-growing businesses, home businesses and Internet businesses, respectively.

- **General interest magazines** — *U.S. News and World Report, Good Housekeeping* and *The Atlantic* often run business and economy trend stories and profiles, but also are most likely to run exposés, consumer service stories and product-benefit stories.

- **Major metropolitan newspapers** — These cover city, regional and national news and trends, usually on a daily basis. Most are very interested in profiling local businesses, especially if they are particularly innovative or if executives yield interesting insights on broad business, societal or economic trends.

- **Local and community newspapers** — With typically daily or weekly circulation, these publications are interested in local companies specifically because they are local. These papers often are the most widely read in their own target markets.

- **Radio stations** — These come in a huge array of formats from news radio to jazz. News/talk, consumer advice and call-in shows often highlight businesspeople who can offer pithy advice to listeners.

- **Local television stations** — Like local papers, these concentrate mainly on local news. Visuals are, of course, very important to television reporters, so the more visually intriguing your product, service or demonstration is, the more likely they are to be interested.

- **Network television news, newsmagazines and talk shows** — These formats tend to cover business in the same manner as general interest newsstand magazines. They usually focus on consumer exposés and how-to stories, as well as companies that exemplify a national trend.

- **Industry specific web sites** — Often called vertical portals, these are ramping up their own coverage of industries. While some are simply licensing editorial content from affiliated trade magazines, others, especially investment and consumer advice sites, are developing their own independent platoons of reporters and editors.

By now, you've probably got a mental list of the media most influential with *your* target market. In fact, you probably used many of these media as sources when you were researching your market and competitors.

# DEVELOPING A MEDIA CAMPAIGN

It can be hard to grab the attention of perennially harried reporters and editors—and even harder to keep their attention, and harder still to successfully pitch a story to them. The way to do it? *Come up with a unique angle that not only presents your company as distinct and different, but that also offers a direct benefit to the reporter's audience.* The fact that your small business exists is neither exciting, nor is it news, nor does it present a direct benefit to the vast majority of readers. Ten-year anniversaries aren't much more compelling, unless you have overcome extraordinary odds to keep your company going (such as surviving multiple natural disasters, personal illnesses or other traumas).

Because you're constantly watching your market for emerging trends, you may be in a great position to point out those trends to a reporter.

For instance, machine-shop operators often detect shifts in local economies as other manufacturers expand or shrink their own production capacity. Informed observations like these can be converted to valuable leads for local reporters.

Still, your company as a whole will gain coverage only if you suggest story ideas that are both timely and relevant to readers. June is a great time to suggest a story on home-security devices because so many people are gearing up for vacation trips. By August, most of those folks are home from their trips and attention is on back-to-school, not empty houses.

You may have to develop two parallel media campaigns, one for the industry and the other for consumers. If innovations in home-security devices are unveiled in at an annual fall trade show, you'll want to send press releases and pictures of your latest device to the appropriate trade magazines that are read by store buyers. Local newspapers, though, that reach readers who actually buy the devices for their homes, should get consumer-oriented press releases about home security in May and June.

## Work Smart

*The trade and consumer press will be interested in your product or service for very different reasons. Though your company backgrounder and executive bios will remain the same, much of the other material in your press kit will change.*

- *Trade magazines want to know all the technical details of your product. They want to know not just what it does, but how it does it. Without being overwhelming, do take the space to clearly explain the technology or process that underlies your new introduction. Tell also how it relates to prior and future products you offer, and specifically what features the product or service has that competitors do not. Direct customer benefits still should be highlighted in the main press release, with technical details following in the same release or perhaps in a tech spec sheet.*

- *Consumer magazines, on the other hand, simply want to know what the product will do for people who buy it, how much it costs and where it is available. If the technology is very unusual (think of how the Internet was explained in 1994), a summary paragraph that quickly and simply explains the underlying technology might be included. However, product benefits will far overshadow features.*

- *Trade magazines will want lots of follow-up information as new versions of your product are introduced and its performance is tracked. They may do a series of stories on your product or service, especially if it changes the way customers do their business or results in dramatic savings.*

- *Consumer magazines aren't likely to mention a product or service more than once every year to 15 months—and then only when brand extensions are added.*

- *Trade magazines may routinely include contact information so that readers can reach you.*

- *Consumer magazines may include a toll-free phone number or a web address, but they are unlikely to list all the ways that a potential customer might contact you. If you have a branded product that is rapidly growing in popularity, consider adding several phone company directory assistance and yellow pages listings under the brand and product category so that customers can find you. Position the brand name prominently on your web site, too, and register it with search engines so that searching surfers can find it.*

- *Trade magazines are much more likely to run a straightforward picture of the product. It's worth while to have a professional photographer take color slides and prints, and black and white prints, to include in the trade version of the press kit.*

- *Consumer magazines usually don't run unadorned product shots. If they're interested in a picture, they're more likely to assign a photographer and model to provide a backdrop, arrange the product in a setting, or show it being used. They may need samples of the product to complete the shoot; deliver the samples at your own expense and expect that they will be handled and marked up during the shoot and therefore not returned.*

As you formulate news and trend angles, ask yourself, "Why does this audience care?" If you can't answer that question quickly and succinctly, you may not have the right angle for the right audience through the right media outlet.

One time-honored way to gain credibility with your target audience is to become an expert source or commentator. Our home-security device manufacturer, for instance, might do additional research on crime statistics during peak vacation weeks, thereby becoming a valued source for reporters.

Once you've chosen the appropriate media, call and ask for an editorial calendar, which outlines the special sections and seasonal topics that editors know in advance they'll be covering. Examine the masthead—the list of editors and their titles. Don't hesitate to call the managing editor to quickly find out which reporters or editors should be receiving your materials. (Start a media database and update it regularly.)

Plot out new product introductions, seasonal or regularly scheduled events (such as conferences or trade shows), and other points on the calendar that provide a bit of a news angle for your upcoming announcements. Note on the calendar how far in advance each of your target media outlets needs to receive material—national special-interest magazines, for instance, usually plan their issues six months in advance of the publication date; assign reporters feature stories five months in advance and allow them a month to be researched and written; allow two to four weeks for the stories to be edited, fact-checked and the graphics developed; and then ship them to the printer about 7 weeks before the publication date. Knowing when the editors and reporters are working on particular topics will enable you to deliver the right information to them at the right time.

## Work Smart

*Being interviewed on a television or radio show can be loads of fun. It's also nerve-racking. Here are some tips to help you make the best impression:*

- *Practice injecting more energy into your voice while speaking slightly more slowly than you would normally. Soft-spoken people need to infuse their speaking style with excitement, lest their audience tunes out. Naturally effervescent types need to make sure they're speaking clearly and precisely, lest they get carried away with their own enthusiasm.*

- *Watch or listen to the program for several days preceding your appearance so you have a feel for the host, call-in questioners and pace of the show.*

- *Bring notes, printed large, on 3 x 5 cards—especially if you'll be referring to statistics, such as industry growth rates or legislation.*

- *Practice making your key points in short, 30-second or-less sound bites.*

- *If you're to appear on television, wear medium-toned, solid-color, classic clothes. Bright white, stripes and dots create unintended special effects when viewed through a television camera and monitor.*

# Elements of a Media Kit

Now's the time to create a media kit that contains all the background information a reporter will need to quickly become familiar with your company, mission statement, products, services, target market and how you help your customers. Contact information, including address, phone, fax and e-mail, should appear on each page of a press release.

- **Company backgrounders** — These summarize, in two to three pages, the history of the company's founding, its target markets, relevant industry statistics, growth plans and primary product lines. Include brands and official trademarks and slogans.

- **Executive biographies** — These are short summaries of the relevant backgrounds of your company's principals. Not only will this help reporters understand the your qualifications, but editors and fact-checkers will rely on bios and backgrounders to make sure that names are spelled right, alma maters properly cited, and other details correct.

- **Press releases** — These convey your news. New products, entering new markets, signing a major contract that will propel you into a new category, reaching a major sales milestone (you'll have to divulge the numbers on that one), and other major changes are in the top paragraphs. Quickly segue into exactly how the news will benefit your target audience; for instance, a new cellular phone service that provides seamless round-the-globe service is high-priced but means that even Antarctic explorers are only a phone call away. How much more convenient will the service be to fishing- and golf-addicted executives who want to simultaneously explore the outdoors and stay in touch with the office?

# Press Etiquette

News media are under constant pressure to report fascinating stories accurately, in very little time. Inevitably, they'll follow-up on the press release that you sent out weeks ago just as you're having a super-busy day. Take the time anyway to talk with reporters; if you don't, they will simply move on to the next likely source on their list so that they can complete their research in time to meet their deadline. If you don't have time for reporters when you're busy, then they will be much less receptive to your pitches and requests for coverage.

Few reporters will let sources review, much less approve, a copy of the story before it goes to print. It's fine to request that the reporter read back direct quotes attributed to you, but don't expect to be re-interviewed. And keep in mind that you're only one of several, possibly dozens, of people being interviewed just for one story. If you're disappointed that only one or two sentences from your half-hour conversation were quoted in the story, rest assured that there are plenty of people interviewed who weren't mentioned at all.

Finally, if you believe you've been misquoted, deliberately or by mistake, write a polite e-mail or note to the reporter correcting the mistake in a straightforward way. Reporters don't want mistakes in their stories, so most will appreciate the chance to set the record straight in the corrections column of the publication.

## Contents of a Press Kit

*A complete press kit will equip reporters with much of the basic information they need to do a thorough job of understanding and writing about your company. The essential elements of a press kit include:*

*A Company Backgrounder page that explains the industry and the competitive positioning of the company—what it does differently and better than its competitors, and what its mission is.*

*An Executive Bios page that explains who is making this happen. Qualifications of company leaders are important indicators of the company's depth, credibility and likelihood of success.*

*A Frequently Asked Questions page that anticipates questions people might ask as they familiarize themselves with the company and start to understand what it's all about.*

FOR IMMEDIATE RELEASE
For additional information contact:

Stacy Smith 617/520-9120
smith@collaborative.com
Melanie Wilcox 617/520-9134
wilcox@collaborative.com
Collaborative Communications, Inc.

## firstsource.com to Launch Auction Service from FairMarket, Inc.

*FairMarket Partnership with ZDNet will Expose firstsource.com to Millions of New Auction Customers*

**Santa Ana, California -- April 19th, 1999 --** firstsource.com, a leading Internet reseller and direct marketer of computer products and wholly-owned subsidiary of En Pointe Technologies, Inc. (NASDAQ: ENPT), announced today that it will launch FairMarket's web auction service on its online superstore, www.firstsource.com. By utilizing Merchant AuctionPlace from FairMarket, Inc., customers will be able to participate in the online auction experience as they bid on computer products at http://auctions.firstsource.com beginning in mid-May. firstsource.com will gain additional exposure to its product listings due to FairMarket's existing marketing relationships with several online communities, including the 18th largest site on the Web, ZDNet (http://auctions.zdnet.com).

"With the growing interest in online auctions, our partnership with FairMarket will assist us in providing a new shopping experience that capitalizes on this demand, offering our customers the opportunity to bid for computer products." said Bob Din, Chairman and CEO of En Pointe Technologies. "Contributing to our decision to partner with FairMarket was their auction relationship with ZDNet who will, through their portal, expose firstsource.com and our new auction site to millions of new shoppers."

The FairMarket Merchant AuctionPlace is a customizable web auction service that enables web-based merchants, such as firstsource.com, to auction current merchandise, excess products or returned items quickly and easily, to registered users. The Merchant AuctionPlace service will

400 Unicorn Park Drive
Woburn, MA 01801
Tel 781.935.7090
Fax 781.935.4575
www.fairmarket.com

FairMarket

*A News Release page that outlines the actual news the company is announcing. The first paragraph contains all the crucial information—what the company is doing, when it was doing it, and how customers will benefit. Occupying the second paragraph is a comment from a test user of the product about how he has already found it useful. The next paragraph launches into a product description—now that we know how the product can help customers, let's find out more about what it is.*

## Case Study — Rudolf, Cinnamon & Calafato

 *Sharon Metz is a spinmeister par excellence. In her first 13 months as marketing director for a Pennsylvania firm, she managed to get her employer mentioned in local and regional newspapers no fewer than 65 times. And her employer is, of all things, a certified public accounting firm, Rudolf, Cinnamon & Calafato.*

*You might think that a CPA firm would be last on a newspaper reporter's list of places to look for exciting news. And you'd be right. But newspapers regularly run service pieces—articles that dole out how-to advice on topics ranging from organizing recipes to choosing investment software for managing the family estate. Financial management topics are a source of constant concern to readers, and reporters are in a state of perpetual worry that they get the facts right, especially if they don't routinely cover finances and investing.*

*Knowing all this, Metz found it easy to position the principals in her firm as experts. She interviewed all senior staffers on their areas of particular expertise and produced short profiles of them for a media guide booklet. It not only helps reporters quickly find the individual who's most likely to answer their questions on a particular topic, but also lists the staffers' home and cell phone numbers and e-mail addresses.*

*With the media guides distributed to local reporters, Metz trained her senior staffers on the nuances of being interviewed. She helped them memorize several versions of the company's mission statement, a 30-second version of its history, and how to quickly extract reader-relevant sound bites from complex tax, investment and financial management issues. (They had, as many executives do, a tendency to drone on in industryese, instead of succinctly driving home points relevant to most readers.)*

*Then Metz trained her sights on local media. Her goal was to make Rudolph, Cinnamon a household name in roughly a 25-mile radius. So, though one of the firm's partners was once interviewed on a national television talk show, she concentrated on cultivating good relationships with the reporters and editors who had the most control over the firm's target market.*

*When a reporter called, on deadline, needing to be walked through the ramifications of a complex piece of retirement-account legislation, Metz and a firm partner dropped everything to help the newspaper develop a graph that clearly outlined the main points of the new law. Not coincidentally, the story was also illustrated with a large picture of the partner who was so helpful.*

*No firm accomplishment is too small to trumpet, from additional services to the sailing trophy won by a staffer. Now, Rudolph, Cinnamon really is a household name in its market—at least, judging from the steady stream of new clients who say they read about the firm in the paper.*

## Sample Timeline for Media Relations Campaign

*Two months before new product introduction and launch:*

- *Update corporate backgrounder.*

- *Start with product descriptions and benefits.*

- *Outline graphic treatment for illustrating product.*

- *Choose what media should receive this material (culled from preexisting list of media contacts maintained by the firm).*

*One month before:*

- *Begin to set up appointments for briefings with key media and industry analysts.*

- *Schedule daily and broadcast media first (because their deadlines are most pressing) and fill in with monthlies and other media (whose deadlines may or may not be more flexible during the product introduction week).*

- *Collect reviews and comments from first draft of product descriptions.*

- *Finalize feature/benefit document and graphic; move to production.*

*Two weeks before:*

- *Brief company spokespeople on both specifics and benefits of products, and on how to work with the media.*

*One week before:*

- *Send completed press kits to selected media.*

*Week of product launch:*

- *Conduct product briefings/demonstrations with media and industry analysts, via in-person, teleconference and phone interviews.*

*End of week:*

- *News reports start to appear. Keep track with clips and tapes.*

*Subsequently:*

- *Continue to answer questions from media about product features/benefits*

- *Follow-up with requested material from magazines on longer deadlines*

- *Follow-up with customer success stories that illustrate the return on investment they gained through using your product or service*

(Source: Collaborative Communications, www.collaborative.com)

## Potential Pitfall

*Disasters are bad enough when they happen to someone else. When your business is at the eye of the storm, it's hard to know how to react. That's why it's important to draw up a communications contingency plan you can fall back on.*

*Public relations disasters range from owning a local deli that sickens hundreds with its salmonella-infected chicken salad to learning from a reporter that one of your employees has been arrested for driving the company car while drunk.*

*Your first and most essential crisis management strategy: Tell the truth, consistently and constantly. Don't try to hide—if determined reporters can't find you, they'll turn to your neighbors and competitors for comments about your situation. It's best to respond courteously and, always, promptly to media inquiries. Formulate a strategy to deal with inquiries and stick with it.*

- *Of course, your first priority is to cooperate with law enforcement officials and investigators.*

- *Temporarily rearrange duties to free up a top executive to serve as the official spokesperson with law enforcement and the media.*

- *Explain to all other employees that they must not make comments of any sort, in the workplace or as "private citizens" to reporters.*

- *Keep a log of all inquiries, interviews and the resulting coverage. Keep a scrapbook of the stories. You may need to defend your response.*

- *Try not to be goaded into divulging confidential information to a reporter, such as the contents of an arrested employee's last performance review.*

- *Remember that there is no such thing as "off the record." Your entire company may come under the media microscope, from the perceived safety of the parking lot at midnight to your off-the-cuff comment that is ripe for misinterpretation.*

- *Formulate statements for employees, investors, customers and suppliers, if you believe they will be worried about how the disaster will affect them. Post it on your web site, broadcast it, fax it or e-mail it, and make sure each employee has a copy so that he can answer questions that outsiders may ask.*

- *When the air has cleared, analyze the impact to your company image, products, business relationships, customer base and employees.*

- *Thank those who patiently stuck with you during the crisis.*

# COMMUNITY RELATIONS

Most consumers harbor an unspoken assumption that local corporations can be good neighbors by supporting charities, community development and local fundraisers. Whether or not such efforts will directly benefit your company depends on what you do; a ball bearing manufacturer simply may not need to have a high profile locally. However, being a good sport and ponying up to help out worthy groups and causes at least can earn your company a reputation for being a decent corporate citizen—and that reputation may prove invaluable when you're recruiting employees, petitioning the zoning committee for a variance, or calming neighbors annoyed with a sudden increase in truck deliveries

## It Worked for Them!

Community service actually can be profitable. Just ask Californian Ann Ruethling. She launched a mail-order catalog of children's books in 1982. The Chinaberry catalog has since developed a loyal following of millions, largely based on Ruethling's first-person comments about the books she carries, all of which are hand-picked by her.

In the early 1990s, Ruethling noticed that customers were asking if Chinaberry might be able to help them organize and run school book fairs, with a portion of the profits benefiting the parents' groups of the sponsoring schools. Ruethling created a book fair division that works with the parent groups to custom-select books on the topics and in the price ranges suitable for the school's population. The books are inventoried and shipped to the schools, where volunteers organize and run the fair, and then reinventory and ship back the remainders.

The result: Parents are exposed to an unusually appealing selection of books; students are encouraged to read; the parents' groups earn thousands for their projects; and Chinaberry sells books profitably while extending its brand into the heart of its target market.

Many companies can come up with similar ventures that let them do well by doing good. Consider:

- creating an internship program for high school students or local college students that capitalizes on particular interests, such as learning computer graphics programs or performing medical lab tests

- guest teaching at local schools about elements of your job, company or industry

- sponsoring youth activities that also benefit the community, such as neighborhood cleanup days

- underwriting very specific projects that are closely tied to your company and create a logical link in customers' minds, such as a sporting goods shop backing a bicycle safety training program for elementary school children or a hospital donating a van to a senior citizens' center

As your company becomes better known, you may be asked to serve on committees of various sorts. It's easy to become overwhelmed with helping good causes from Little League to cancer prevention. Some companies set aside an annual budget for doling out time, money and in-kind donations, and distribute it on a first-come, first-served basis. Others solicit employees' opinions about what causes and community efforts to support, and then politely turn down all other requests.

# Special Events

Retailers and consumer service companies are well positioned to participate in community, supplier and customer special events. Look for opportunities to draw attention to your location by offering to host public meetings in your cafeteria, say, or inviting the local high school's computer club to surf on your T-1 lines once a month.

Set up an event calendar or diary for your business—the kind with big squares you can scribble in. Note all opportunities for events as the year progresses and when your customers may be observing special events, such as the local senior citizens' group birthday party. When those dates near, you can take the lead in offering to plan and host the events. Watch your local papers and church bulletins for events you didn't get to participate in this year, but will not want to miss selling to next year.

With community events, you may find that generosity to one group touches off a domino effect of requests from other groups. The more visible you are in the community—retail stores, restaurants and banks are particularly affected—the greater the chance that you'll be approached repeatedly to underwrite events.

When you've done one or two and have evaluated the value of those events to your overall marketing efforts, take a step back and develop a strategy for how to handle the inevitable rush of additional requests. If you're in a small town or tightly knit community, confer with employees about how they'd like to see your company positioned with your neighbors. Employees may have some great ideas for choosing one or two events to sponsor that will yield maximum exposure for your company.

Sponsoring a business event involves a different set of considerations. You will, of course, want to know exactly who is attending and then figure out how closely the attendees align with your target market. Sponsorships take many different forms, from simply having a "friends of" line in the event program to scoring major publicity points if sponsoring companies are profiled in the organization's newsletter. Be sure to find out what you're getting for your money. And remember: If you're on a major committee or board of a business group, you probably will be expected to underwrite some parts of some events, such as sponsoring a table at the annual awards banquet.

### Work Smart

*Participating in community efforts or sponsoring special events may cost more than you initially anticipate. Here are some factors to keep in mind.*

- *How much time will it take to prepare for the event?*

- *Does the timing coincide with a crunch time in your work flow? You may be forced to hire temporary workers or pay overtime to serve your customers while still fulfilling your event commitment.*

- *Will you be expected to pay additional money to support event advertising in local papers or for joint services such as trash pickup after the event?*

- *What special publicity or promotional materials will you have to produce just for this event? You may, for instance, have to rent a booth and have a special weatherproof sign made just for outdoor summertime community events. As well, you may want to have extra brochures on hand to give away. How will you dispose or store special materials from event to event?*

- *Does your participation require any special technology, such as electrical service to the middle of a public park?*

- *What materials do you have on hand that can be reused? Some companies give away key chains, pens, magnets and other promotional items.*

- *Who will actually represent you at the event? Will you need to compensate employees with comp time or pay overtime because they worked on a weekend?*

- *Will you actually be selling anything at the event? If so, you'll have to have cash, credit card acceptance technology, inventory, staffers and event security all lined up.*

- *Is it appropriate to include a drawing, raffle or other promotional program at the event?*

- *Can you cut costs by cooperating with another local business that also targets the same market, but for a different product or service? For instance, a workout gym might co-sponsor a booth at a local community fair where people can get a blood pressure reading with a local doctor's practice.*

- *How will you collect and then follow-up on names of people who want more information about your company?*

# PROFESSIONAL RELATIONS

Networking isn't just for energetic sales types. By getting to know others in your local business community and your industry, you'll learn from other businesses, make contacts that may turn into solid sales leads, and sharpen your communications skills. At the very least, you'll get plenty of opportunities to tell people your 15-second spiel about what your company does and how it benefits its customers.

Many Chambers of Commerce and independent business development centers sponsor monthly breakfasts, networking cocktail hours, and community service committees and projects. Find those that best fit your style. If you love circulating and small talk, cocktail parties may be the highlight of your week, while others may prefer the more serious purpose of analyzing legislation with a committee of like-minded souls.

Be aware that different types of events offer different types of networking opportunities. Business groups exist for myriad reasons, and networking is only one.

Fundraising and community events—such as the group hosting an event honoring outstanding teen entrepreneurs—are "softer" social events where your goal is to see and be seen, to mix and become acquainted with various community and business leaders. It's rarely appropriate to aggressively hand out business cards and talk shop under those circumstances. If you do so, you run the risk of appearing socially clueless or desperate for business.

On the other hand, events specifically set up for networking and making purely business connections with others are usually clearly labeled as such. Salesmen's breakfasts are a classic example; local companies each send a representative to the breakfast, where each attendee has three to five minutes to introduce himself, his company and what it does, to others at the same table. Cards are exchanged, notes made, and by 8 a.m. everyone's out the door.

Occupying the fuzzy middle are general business events, workshops, local small business exhibitions, and similar events that have agendas other than pure networking, but that are focused on enhancing business relationships. Be friendly, but not pushy. When in doubt, call the event's organizers ahead of time and ask what the expectations are for networking. Simply explain that you're new to the group or event, and would appreciate a little insight into the typical format and mode of operating.

One often overlooked networking gold mine is your own business advisory board. Whether you have a formal board of advisors or a "kitchen cabinet" of business friends whom you call on when you need a dose of good advice, they can be your most effective advocates. Those who know you, your company, and your business ethics very well are best situated to open the door for you with new customers. They not only can articulate your mission in a way that a new casual acquaintance cannot, but they also make a powerful endorsement when they put their own reputations on the line when recommending you. Advisory board members can keep their ears to the ground for opportunities for you—for instance, advisors to a printing company may have an inside line on what local businesses are expanding and therefore are in imminent need of additional graphics services and printed materials.

Of course, you'll also be doing the same for them. Networking is a two-way street—you'll get as good as you give.

When meeting new people, always be prepared to discuss your company and how you help your customers. Consider these tips:

- Have a few business cards handy in every wallet or purse you use.

- Keep a few sets of brochures and marketing materials (in an envelope, to keep them in pristine condition) in your car, briefcase, carry-on luggage and home office, so you're always prepared to hand it out to interested people.

- Don't overwhelm new acquaintances with details of your company's offerings and business war stories. Instead, listen to their response to your explanation of your company's mission and let them ask for more information.

- Dish out free advice when asked. People love to pick the brains of experts—and that's how you'll be seen.

- Remember, you may make valuable contacts with people who aren't potential clients. You might meet the owner of another small company with whom you could cross-market coupons to each other's customers.

- Before you contact a social acquaintance with a sales call, ask the potential prospect's permission to start a business conversation.

- Use an automated contact management program (such as GoldMine or Act!) that enables you to keep track of the specific preferences and needs of current and potential clients.

## Case Study — Wilson McHenry Co.

 *Julie McHenry knows all about the apocryphal tale of the shoemaker's children who went barefoot. More than a few employees have pointed out to the chief executive officer of the California high-tech media relations firm Wilson McHenry Co. that the firm could use a dose of its own medicine.*

*The trouble was, McHenry herself was so busy formulating media strategies for her ever-expanding list of clients that she just didn't have time to come up with her own plan. A solution came in the form of employee Doniece Sandoval, who wanted to branch out to form her own media relations boutique. McHenry tossed Sandoval her first piece of business: analyzing Wilson McHenry's current media relations materials, developing a strategic plan and then enacting it.*

*The first thing Sandoval determined was that Wilson McHenry's materials were graphically erratic. New brochures and parts of the web site were added to describe new products and services, but no one had been in charge of overseeing the overall effort. Sandoval recommended a complete overhaul of all the graphic and printed materials, starting with a freshened logo.*

*McHenry was intrigued by the company's success with its annual blowout client party, which brought together dozens of Silicon Valley hotshots for a day-long seminar on industry trends followed by a hearty party. Clients constantly referred to the great leads they made during the event and commented that they felt that they often didn't get much out of industry prognosticators' speeches—but always learned something from the speakers that McHenry roped in.*

*Sandoval and McHenry decided to capitalize on McHenry's instinct for choosing timely topics and position her as an expert media strategist and troubleshooter for high-tech companies. They researched and developed several topics of interest to the fast-growth media companies that McHenry considered her most lucrative base of potential customers. Sandoval made her pitch to meeting planners for small business advisory and specialized industry groups within an 80-mile radius. Hungry for fresh faces and voices to fill their meeting schedules, many were happy to sign up McHenry—especially because she didn't charge.*

*A year after the speech strategy was launched, McHenry says she's more than happy with the results. She now makes two to four speeches a month to wholly new audiences and is starting to see corporate clients come on board as a direct result.*

Chapter **11**

# Are You Getting What You're Paying For?

There's an old saying that only half of the money you spend on marketing actually works—but you don't know which half.

It can be hard to get a handle on exactly what you're getting for your marketing investment—the **return on investment** (ROI). Some marketing tools, like coupons and direct mail, are self-reporting. A coupon redemption rate of 5 percent is great; you definitely gained customers. However, many efforts will be harder to track. If your company's revenues grew 10 percent last year, was that the result of several well-placed speeches you made or your revamped, multi-part brochure? More than likely, some audience members were persuaded to call just because of your speech; others were most influenced by the brochure; and yet others didn't hear the speech but were told by those that did that you were knowledgeable.

Nevertheless, you don't want to just guess at which methods are working best. You want all the feedback you can get so that you can sharpen your pitch to your most profitable base of loyal customers and expand that base.

Get into the habit of building a **response mechanism** into each individual effort. Ask customers who stroll into your store how they found out about it—through seeing the sign, by reading your ads or from attending the local charity auction to which you'd donated a set of golf clubs? Give employees a form that lists the possibilities (drawn from your current and past marketing campaigns), so they can prompt customers who are fuzzy on the details of just how they became aware of your existence. Include response postcards with products or leave them behind when your company has completed a service contract.

Regardless of the particular marketing tool—advertising, promotion, media relations and so on—that you're measuring, you'll want to find out:

- if awareness of your company has increased—that is, if more people know that you exist

- if awareness has increased of the benefits of the products and services you offer; do people know why you exist and how you might benefit them?

- if the brand or corporate image you're cultivating is getting through

- if you're reaching the right audience (despite the assurances of the eager media salesperson, the classical radio station you love may not actually reach the teenagers you want to attract to your video game parlor)

- if the message you're using to reach that audience persuades them try out your product or service

- if the price you're charging is considered fair, a rip-off or a steal

- if people can get your product or service conveniently

- if they are recommending your company to their friends, co-workers or other decision makers

You'll soon learn which tools deliver which results. Then you can evaluate the effectiveness of the marketing campaign by comparing the amount you spent on it with the benefit you gained. If you're simply trying to create awareness of your new computer screen glare shield, you may be thrilled to learn that the barrage of direct mail you sent to potential customers before a trade show resulted in dozens of retail buyers stopping by your booth—even if you didn't get any sales on the spot.

On the other hand, if you used direct mail to pitch the glare shields to managers of customer service call centers, you'll want to compare the amount you spent on the direct-mail campaign to the gross revenues and net profits you reaped from orders placed as a result.

## Potential Pitfall

*What you've accomplished is not the same as what you've done. Activity doesn't necessarily equal results. Completing every item on a marketing goals checklist—hired an ad agency to concoct an ad and paying the local newspaper to run it on page 6 every Thursday—is what you've done.*

*Remember, the purpose of the marketing activity is what you hope to accomplish, not just the activity itself. If the newspaper ads draw in 15 new customers weekly, and 10 of them buy an average of $25 worth of goods, then you've gained $250 in sales weekly because of the ads. They've accomplished the purpose of expanding your customer base.*

*To be sure, stay on track with the activities on your marketing to-do list—but also track, separately, what those activities have accomplished towards your overall marketing plan and strategy.*

# CULTIVATE YOUR MOST PROFITABLE MARKET

It's more than possible to gain market share but lose money in the process—companies do it all the time by pricing their products so low that they gain lots of customers, but can't even recoup the cost of producing the product or providing the service.

That's not a very healthy long-term strategy. Strictly speaking, it can't even be a long-term strategy—only a short-term one. Still, you'll find that your customers fall into four categories (see graph below). Some of those customers may help boost your market share, but they're actually not worth the bother. Very demanding customers that constantly try to negotiate special discounts just for them; that return merchandise extremely frequently; and that are always taxing the time and patience of your customer service staffers, salespeople and others who have to solve their complex problems may be costing you far more than the sales volume they bring in.

**Customer Profitability Matrix**

| | |
|---|---|
| *Customers you make money on, frequently* | *Customers you make money on, infrequently* |
| *Customers you lose money on, frequently* | *Customers you lose money on, infrequently* |

Seek ways to deepen the loyalty of frequently profitable customers by:

- cultivating close, constant communication with them

- creating spin-offs and different versions of products they like

- working hard to anticipate their needs, market trends and buying motivations so you can continue to earn their loyalty

Ask yourself why customers from whom you occasionally profit don't buy your product or service more often.

- What alternatives to your product or service do they use when they aren't using yours?

- What adjustments to the design, pricing, packaging or distribution, or to your product or service, might persuade these occasional buyers to shift their buying loyalty to you?

Why are you losing money on business with some customers, occasionally?

- What adjustments to the design, pricing, packaging or distribution, or to your product or service, might result in profits? For instance, if this customer consistently places orders so late in your production cycle that you have to pay workers overtime to complete it by deadline, might you create an e-mail order form to eliminate time-consuming paperwork and get the order sooner?

- Are there trends emerging in the market that are affecting this category of customers first, but that might soon spread to your profitable customers?

Why do you continue to do business with customers that nearly always result in money-losing transactions?

- Are there mitigating factors—perhaps the customer is extremely influential with other, profitable, customers—that make it worthwhile for non-financial reasons to keep this customer on?

- What glitches in your operation might be at odds with the process of serving this customer so that you always lose money?

- Are your salespeople so eager to gain market share that they're giving away the store? Educate them on the financial impact of making any deal just to get the sale.

- Does this customer have characteristics that won't change, that you can't compensate for, such as being located in a foreign country?

- If you dropped this customer, what might be the ramifications on your company image and industrial relationships, as well as with colleagues?

# DEVELOP A PRO-ACTIVE MARKETING STRATEGY

Just because others in your market category have always advertised in certain trade journals or gotten a front-page picture of their Christmas window display in the local newspaper, doesn't mean that you can't break out of the mold.

If you've carefully examined your market and you truly believe that you can market your products in a completely new, fresh way that will add value to customers, don't hesitate to try out your new idea. You may be able to persuade a media or distribution outlet to give you a big price break on your experiment, if you promise to share the results with them and buy more space or time, or channel volumes of goods through them, if your hunch proves correct.

## It Worked for Them!

When Maddie and Frank Slonka started thinking about leveraging Frank's thirty-plus years in the steel fabricating business, they first thought about his technical expertise in shaping thin sheets of metal into products and components of products for home centers and manufacturers.

Then, they worried about getting the $75,000 they needed to acquire the materials and pay for the shop they'd have to rent.

Only after they had figured out how they could make a go of their new company, Dominion Steel, Inc., did it dawn on them that they'd also need to do some marketing. When they did start thinking about it, the Slonkas' task seemed daunting. Because Dominion does custom fabrication of steel according to customers' drawings, it was hard to pinpoint just one or two categories of potential buyers. Everyone from local boat manufacturers to roofers might be their customers.

They started by putting together a basic target list simply by combing through the Yellow Pages and creating a database of possible customers. Then, they joined several industry groups, in the hopes of gaining some work from larger competitors on the fringe of their market. As well, they joined the local Chamber of Commerce so that they'd become familiar with local business owners and executives—and so that other Chamber members would already have heard of Dominion when they heard or saw a reference to the new company.

The Slonkas' first sales strategy was to just position Dominion as a local and convenient steel fabricating center. At the time, the nearest competitor was at least 45 miles away. Simple convenience, though, wasn't much of an incentive for potential customers to abandon the fabricators with whom they'd been doing business for years. For three months, the Slonkas had not a single sale.

Finally, a few local customers started tossing emergency, last-minute jobs to Dominion. Of course, by then they recognized the Slonkas from their repeated sales calls. Dominion's sign, which can be seen from a local highway, drew in a few additional customers.

*Things really picked up when the Slonkas hired an outside sales rep whose only job was to open doors, warm up prospects and leave brochures about Dominion's services. Then, the Slonkas would follow-up. Even though it takes an average of five sales contacts to close the first sale, the Slonkas believed that if they could just showcase their services once they'd have that customer hooked.*

*They were right. Three years after it opened, Dominion Steel employed 11 people and had $1.4 million in annual sales. Persistence paid off.*

Staying one step ahead of your customers so that they're encountering your products or services just as they're realizing they need it will build your credibility as a knowledgeable supplier. Anticipating their needs may be as simple as a popular lunch spot offering a fax-order and delivery service to surrounding office buildings.

Marketing is nothing more than a long-term conversation with people to whom you're selling goods and services that make their lives easier, more comfortable, more fulfilled, or more fun. As you continue to hone your marketing expertise, don't lose sight of the individual customer relationships you're developing. Whether you're selling a mass-produced toy or customized software, each buyer wants to know that he's important to you.

## Worksheet: ANNUAL MARKETING PLAN

*What is the objective of your plan (how does this further your overall business goals)?* _____

_____

_____

*What is the overall marketing budget?* _____

_____

_____

*What are the primary categories of marketing spending (sales compensation, research, advertising, etc.)?* _____

_____

_____

*What are the secondary categories of marketing spending (how you'll spend additional money, if available)?* _____

_____

_____

*Who are your target customers (list the categories of prospects you want to reach; include a few key characteristics that indicate why they will benefit from your products or services)?* _____

_____

_____

*For each category of prospect:*

- *What are the top three ways of reaching these prospects?* _____
  _____

- *How much would each type of marketing campaign cost to effectively reach this audience?* _____
  _____

- *How does this fit into the overall marketing budget?* _____
  _____

- *Which is the best one for the current situation and goals?* _____
  _____

- *How do the efforts to reach this audience reinforce each other (for instance, what percentage of the sales staff's time will be devoted to following up on a direct mail campaign)?* _____
  _____

- *What is the current penetration into the market category (establish a benchmark; otherwise, you won't know how much of a difference the marketing campaign has made)?* _____
  _____

- *How will success be defined with this market (how much additional sales must you get from this category to feel that your marketing campaign was a success, or is there another measure of success that you might use, such as referrals)?* _____
  _____

- *How much will the campaign cost?* _____
  _____

- *How long will the campaign last?* _____
  _____

- *What is the return on investment (how much will you gain in additional sales, and additional profits, from this category, compared to the amount of money you spent to win these customers—if you spend $5 to attract a customer to your auto wash, and that customer spends $10 getting his car washed, your ROI for that single exchange was $5; if with no additional advertising, the customer returns and spends another $10, your ROI is $15)?* _____
  _____

## Here's a Real-Life Example of How It Works

*A car dealership decided to sponsor a float in its hometown Fourth of July parade.*

*Exposure to thousands of patriotic-feeling observers will reinforce local television and newspaper advertising.*

*Additional marketing expenses might include flyers detailing the dealership's location and offering a case of soda pop in exchange for a test drive by qualified shoppers. The cost of printing and distributing the flyers, as well as the projected cost of the gift pop, must be factored in.*

*The dealership isn't attracting as many new college graduates as it wants. The offer of the pop is designed to attract them.*

*It costs $50 to enter the parade; another $800 to advertise in the booklet listing all the parade participants, which will be handed out to people watching; $1,000 in employee time to prepare the campaign and coordinate the event, including the distribution of flyers; $5,000 to actually provide materials and labor to create the float; a $300 honorarium to the Boy Scout troop that populates the float en route. Total cost to participate in the parade—$7,150.*

*The parade lasts for two hours.*

*In the two weeks after the parade, 25 young adults come in, are qualified for auto loans, and take test drives. They tell your employees that many of their friends are interested in earning a case of soda pop for the not-too-onerous chore of test-driving a car. Word is getting out among your target audience.*

*Five of the young adults buy the cars they test-drive. Your profit on each car is $2,000. The direct return on investment for the parade is $10,000 - $7,150 = $2,850. Of course, many additional people watched the parade, so it's possible that awareness of the dealership has been sufficiently raised to draw in upward of 50 more potential customers, resulting in 10 more actual sales, over the next month.*

## SOME FINAL WORDS

A business is just an idea until it has a steady roster of paying customers. Armed with the information in this book, you're ready to convert your concept into a viable, growing business that readily adapts to customers' ever-changing needs.

As you become more adept at marketing, you'll develop an intuitive sense of what your customers want and need and how you can fulfill those needs in the manner and at the price they're willing to pay—and that turns a profit for you. You'll be The Man Who Marketed Just Right.

# Index

# U

U.S. Patent and Trademark
Office, 78
Underpositioning, 18
Unique
business idea, 4
positioning statement, 8, 41,
65, 67, 68, 76, 144
product or service, 99
USAData, 44

# V

Val-Pak, 156

# W

Wal-Mart Innovation
Network, 49

Web sites, 23, 35, 63, 64, 65,
67, 69, 77, 108, 115, 123,
128, 139, 144, 154, 159, 166,
167, 169, 170, 177, 180
Wholesalers, 102, 108, 111,
113
Worksheets
advertising planning, 177
annual marketing plan, 202
crafting a corporate image
strategy, 67
crafting a product/service
marketing strategy, 68
how will your customers
benefit from purchasing
your product or service?,
40
promotion planning, 176
promotional and advertising
budgeting, 146
shaping your unique
positioning statement, 65
web site planning, 169